Understanding divine intelligence behind

Creation | Time | Relationship | Miracles | Prayer

The 12 Secrets of the Kingdom

Harold Wafo& Dr. Phil Gates

THE 12 SECRETS OF THE KINGDOM

Copyright August 2012

Harold Wafo& Dr. Phil Gates

ISBN-13: 978-0615682891

ISBN-10: 0615682898

Publish in the USA by

BIBLE DISCIPLES

Cover by: Tom Nadeau (I AM Graphic Design)

For further information or permission, address:

BIBLE DISCIPLES

Tel: 240 347 2475 (240 – DISCIPLE)

Contact@bibledisciples.org

www.bibledisciples.org

All Scripture quotation are from the New King James Version of the Bible, except otherwise stated.

Contents

Tomy wifePatricia, this book would never have been written without her permanent and unconditional spiritual and moral support. I love you.

- Harold Wafo

Thank you to all my children, who are are great inspiration to me.

- Dr. Phil Gates

.... It is given unto you to know the mysteries of the kingdom of heaven,....

– Mat 13:11

Introduction

By one count, there are more than thirty-eight thousand Christian denominations. Many people have said that the greatest barrier to becoming a Christian is all the division they see in the church.

God's deepest longing is for the church to be united as one body. In Jesus' longest recorded prayer, he prayed that we would be "one as God is one." As one old preacher said, "We gotta get it together, because Jesus is coming back, and he's coming for a bride, not a harem."

God has only one church. (Common Prayer, A Liturgy for Ordinary Radicals, Shaine Claiborne, Jonathan Wilson-Hartgrove, Enuma Okoro. Zondervan 2010) "There is no

Plan B." (Rich Mullins, Christian songwriter, poet, artist, prophet)

It was not until I was 17 years old that I started thinking of life after death. I was living a "good" life. I had all I wanted, but I started thinking, "What if when I die it is different?" Deep inside me, I knew that life after the grave was a reality. I don't know how, but I was very sure about that. I was not a Christian; I was not going to church, and none of my family was involved in any way with church activities. I started asking questions of any person I knew as 'spiritual' about life after the grave. I read many books, and I came across many doctrines like reincarnation, complete annihilation, purgatory, resurrection, hell, heaven, and so on. It was all very confused in my young mind. For some reason I was determined to prepare for my life after the grave. I can't explain why. It is a mystery.

Something came to my mind. "If you want to know about Paris, just ask to somebody who has been there. If you want to know about New York, just ask to somebody who has been there." I suddenly realized that the only person I could ask about life after the grave was Jesus. He is the only one who has been there and come back. I asked for a Bible and read the New Testament. I was convinced in my heart by that reading, but I had experience of seeing how the Christian life was taught in church. I said to myself I will never be able to live like "Christians". My interest for spirituality dropped to zero.

On January 21, 1993, I was going out with a friend and encountered an evangelical crusade. A German preacher named Peter Schneider was preaching on the story of Noah. He spoke about the power of Jesus to set us free. I was so touched and moved by the experience. When I went home, I got on my knees and prayed: "Jesus I believe you are the son of God, but I cannot live the life you want. If you change my heart, I will follow the Bible and live the way you want." I confessed my sins in the same prayer, and I asked for forgiveness. I knew for sure I could not stop certain bad habits.

The very same day I went to my cousin's room and asked for a Bible. I told him what I did; his response: "I give you three weeks." When I started to read the Bible, I was so absorbed that I lost all track of time. I was reading an average of six hours a day. The Bible suddenly became alive to me. Everything was so real, and for the first time it was making complete sense. After a couple of months, without noticing, my life was totally transformed. I was surprised myself. I was totally free. I found a great pleasure in living a Christian life. The Bible became true because it caused me to live what it declares. It was a big miracle to me. It was so natural to live and enjoy the Bible.

Very soon I was passionately praying for the salvation of my family. I was involved in many evangelical crusades. I co-founded a Christian group in my university. The fire was ablaze. The passion was great. Without any formal teaching on the subject, I taught that when we are saved, we are delivered from the power of darkness and empowered to live a sinless life. Jesus has done everything; now it is up to us to manifest a Godly life. I understood the grace of God was manifested in salvation. After being saved, I thought, "I can do all things through Christ."

My life was "perfect" from my perspective, and I was told I was a perfect example to others as well. Many friends and family named their children "Harold" after me. This is not a common name in any French colony. I was born in Cameroon, a French colony of central Africa. In a French colony the first name of a child is supposed to be a French name. As I was growing up, I never encountered anyone else with my first name. I asked my father one day why he named me Harold. His response was that he named me after Harold Wilson, the prime minister of the United Kingdom.

When I got saved I experienced a strong rejection from my family as the first believer. I have experienced the presence, the power and the glory of God in prayer. My family became saved, one after another. I attained the highest ranking in my class. Many blessings came to me. I used to say "there is nothing you cannot possess through prayer."

I relocated to the USA. I started developing a great appetite for doctrines. I was attending a Baptist Charismatic Church, and I came to the knowledge of "the Grace of God," learning that everything before and after salvation is done by the grace of God. It made perfect sense to me, but it was in contradiction with the doctrine of faith that I knew. It was also in contradiction with the commands of God in the New Testament. If everything is by the grace of God, then why am I commanded to believe? If everything is done by the grace of God, then why I am even asked to obey? How can God ask of me what I cannot do myself? Going through the scriptures, the grace of God made perfect sense to me.

Without noticing, my prayer life vanished, and soon after I became just a "religious" person, with no passion for the Bible or the things of God. There was no fire for prayer, evangelism, or teaching. I kept the law; I knew what was right and wrong. I got to a point where I could not even pray for 10 minutes. I felt like I had lost God. Horrible things started happening to me. I made the worst decisions of my life. I did things I couldn't have done even before my faith in Christ. I was miserable and felt powerless before my sinful nature.

Then one day a friend of mine invited me to a meeting, I went there just to please her; my heart was not in it. The preacher preached on intimacy with God and anointing. I was very touched. I remembered when I was so intimate with God; I was so familiar with God's voice, His presence, the Holy Spirit. When I could spend night and days with God with no effort, it was so natural.

After the message I prayed, "God I want to come back to you but I can't. I have no desire to pray, no passion for the Bible; bring me back to you, for I am so miserable without you." Strangely, the next time I opened my mouth to pray with my sister at the table before the meal, as soon as I opened my mouth the presence of God could be felt in the room. After a short prayer, she turned to me and asked, "Where have you been? I feel the presence of God so strong."

We started praying each day and night in her house. It was a great revival in the house. Since then, I have experienced a level of presence and fellowship with God that I never knew before.

One day I was talking to God, and I asked Him how it happened that I drifted away from Him. I could not understand how I found myself living without His presence. The Lord revealed to me what I consider to be the greatest revelation of my Christian life: Grace, Faith and Obedience. It opened my eyes to the root cause of denominations and led me to the twelve keys in the Kingdom every believer should possess. In this book I share those with you.

Knowing is not understanding. There is a great difference between knowing and understanding: you can know a lot about something and not really understand it.

-   Charles Kettering

Secret 1

Understanding: A requirement of the Kingdom

Why do I need to understand?

While I was sharing with my wife about the book, she asked me this question "Why do we need to understand all these mysteries?" I smiled and said "very good question" and shared, Jesus said:

> *"But he who received seed on the good ground is he who hears the word and **understands** it, who indeed bears fruit and produces: some a hundredfold, some sixty, some thirty."*   Mat 13:23

A great theologian, Joseph Ratzinger (currently Pope Benedict XVI) has recently written a two-volume book on Jesus of Nazareth. In the first volume he explains his approach in reviewing the scriptures to discern the nature of Jesus. He discusses the great extent of recent interest in using the "historical-critical" method of looking at scripture, and trying by dissecting scripture using this method to "prove" or "disprove" the authenticity of some of the writings. Two important points he makes are that:

1. Scripture must be taken as a whole (that is the New Testament and the Old Testament must be recognized as being a continuous sharing of the story of God's involvement with the lives of His people), and

2. Scripture is inspired by God. "Let us dwell for the time being on the unity of Scripture...This process is certainly not linear, and it is often dramatic, but when you watch it unfold in light of Jesus Christ you can see it moving in a single overall direction; you can see that the Old and New Testaments belong together. This Christological hermeneutic, which sees Jesus Christ as the key to the whole and learns from him how to understand the Bible as a unity, presupposes a prior act of faith. It cannot be the conclusion of a purely historical method. But this act of faith is based upon reason—historical reason —and so makes it possible to see the internal unity of Scripture."

"a voice greater than man's echoes in Scripture's human words; the individual writings of the Bible point somehow to the living process that shapes the one Scripture.... it is necessary to keep in mind that any human utterance of a certain weight contains more than the author may have been immediately aware of at the time. When a word transcends the moment in which it is spoken, it carries within itself a "deeper value." This "deeper value" pertains most of all to words that have matured in the course of faith-history. For in this case the author is not simply speaking for himself on his own authority.

"He is speaking from the perspective of a common history that sustains him and that already implicitly contains the possibilities of its future, of the further stages of its journey. The process of continually rereading and drawing out new meanings from words would not have been possible unless the words themselves were already open to it from within. At this point we get a glimmer, even on the historical level, of what inspiration means: The author does not speak as a private, self-contained subject. He speaks in a living community, that is to say, in a living historical movement not created by him, nor even by the collective, but which is led forward by a greater power that is at work." This underscores the living character of scripture, life being one of the natural characteristics of God: John 14:6 Jesus said to him, "I am the way, and the truth, and the life. No one comes to the Father except through me."

Another important point to remember about Scripture, reflected in the above, is that it is living. And as a living book, the Bible does speak to us in our individual circumstances. The Scripture is the spoken Word of God. When God speaks, He creates.

> "In the beginning God created the heavens and the earth. The earth was without form, and void; and darkness was on the face of the deep. And the Spirit of God was hovering over the face of the waters." Then God said…"
> Gen 1: 1-3

Creation came from God's Word. And in the Gospel of John, we are told the Word became flesh.

> In the beginning was the Word, and the Word was with God, and the Word was God. He was in the beginning with God. All things came into being through him, and without him not one thing came into being. What has come into being in him was life, and the life was the light of all people.
> John 1:1-4

The Word is of course Jesus, it is also Scripture, and it is the creative force of God, through the Holy Spirit. The Word is alive and it is life. It is the way, the truth, and the life.

It is only when you understand the Word that you can bear its fruit. Understanding the Word establishes its content in your life. The Bible is full of mysteries. Many verses make no sense at first look. Many seem to be contradictory. And others simply sound foolish. This is part of the reason we have too many denominations believing the same Book. It is only when you are given the grace to understand, that you take full advantage of it. No wonder we are called stewards of the mysteries of God.

> *Let a man so consider us, as servants of Christ and* ***stewards of the mysteries*** *of God."*   *1 Cor 4:1*

We do not believe because we understand, but we must understand when we believe. When we receive the Word in our spirit and understand it in our soul then the body naturally obeys. We must approach the Word as little children. The Bible is true whether we understand it or not. We can then come humbly before God and pray: Holy Spirit, teach me.

What does that mean: understanding?

The dictionary defines "understand" by: To perceive and comprehend the nature and significance, to take in the meaning, nature, or importance. But I will present understanding in this context as a vehicle that brings knowledge to our soul. When a teacher lectures, He is simply trying to bring knowledge to students by means of understanding. The great commission:

> *"Go therefore and make disciples..." How? "Teaching them..."*   *Mat 28:19-20*

What happens when you don't understand?

> *"When anyone hears the word of the kingdom, and* ***does not understand*** *it, then the* ***wicked one comes and snatches*** *away what was sown in his heart."*   *Mat 13:19*

Salvation must be understood, heaven, hell, love, mercy, etc. Everything found in the Bible should be understood.

> *So shall the knowledge of wisdom be to your soul; If you have found it, there is a prospect, And your* ***hope*** *will not be cut off.*   *Pro 24:14*

The place of understanding in the Gospel

The entire gospel from salvation to perfection revolves around understanding. Understanding a mystery gives you possession of it content. Without understanding there is no knowledge and without knowledge, destruction is unavoidable, for it is written

"My people are destroyed for lack of knowledge. Because you have rejected knowledge, I also will reject you..."   *Hos 4:6*

Today we are not defeated by the devil or sin, nor sickness or the world. We are only destroyed because we lack knowledge.

May the eyes of your understanding be enlightened; that you may know what is the hope of His calling, Eph 1:18

God is alive and He speaks to us today in many ways. Just as I somehow "knew" deep inside of me that life after the grave was a reality, just as my delving deeply into Scripture and going to an evangelical crusade greatly touched my life, God was speaking to me. The critical first step was that I listen.

Be sure that you make everything according to the pattern I have shown you here on the mountain.

- Ex 25:40 NLT

Secret 2

God works with patterns

God works with patterns.

When we look at the world, it is remarkable to see how every creation of God follows a specific pattern. Human beings, plants, animals follow a specific pattern. The heart of every human being has the same parts and performs the same functions. So also are the brain, the eyes regardless of the nation, skin color, or age. The heart of a man is the same everywhere. Sometimes I wonder how the world would be if every human being had his own design. For example, if the heart of each person was different and had a different functionality. God works with patterns. Each species has been created according to a divine pattern. At a functional level, there is uniformity between the creatures of the same species.

When God wanted to have a Tabernacle built for Him to dwell in the midst of the children of Israel, before He gave any instruction on how the tabernacle should be made, He commanded Moses:

> *Make this tabernacle and all its furnishings exactly like the pattern I will show you.*   *Ex 25:9 NIV*

After He gave the plans and details how to build the

tabernacle to Moses, He said again:

> *Be sure that you make everything according to the pattern I have shown you here on the mountain.*
> *Ex 25:40 NLT.*

God works with patterns. To understand how God works, the ways of God, we must know His patterns. When we understand the patterns of God we have a better understanding of the word of God. We can anticipate God's actions. We also understand why some are failing where others are succeeding. We pray strategically, step by step, knowing how God works. For success is not a miracle; it is simply an application of God's principles: working in divine order.

We must understand God's patterns

We are body, soul and spirit. When we know God in our spirit by revelation and we understand the patterns of God in our soul, our body naturally obeys Him without objection.

> *But he who received seed on the good ground is he who hears the word and understands it, who indeed bears fruit and produces: some a hundredfold, some sixty, some thirty."* Mat 13:26

Paul the apostle understood the pattern of divine healing. He knew what it takes to be healed by God.

> *In Lystra a certain man without strength in his feet was sitting, a cripple from his mother's womb, who had never walked. This man heard Paul speaking. Paul, observing him intently and seeing that he had faith to be healed, said with a loud voice, "Stand up straight on your feet!" And he leaped and walked.*
> *Act 19:8-10 NKJV.*

He knew what it takes and what to do to receive a miracle from God. He knew that man would be healed even before he commanded him to stand up straight. He knew God's pattern for healing. On earth God creates only the pattern, the model. Then he places in the model the capability to multiply. The species multiplies according to the model. At a functional level, there is uniformity among the creatures of the same species.

God created Adam and placed in him the capability to reproduce, to multiply. Every other man therefore derived from Adam. Other men are God's creation, but they are simply the multiplication of what God has already done. I believe when Adam sinned, God saw the sins of Adam in every human being on earth. Right then he prophesied the coming of the second Adam, Jesus:

And between your seed and her Seed; He shall bruise your head, and you shall bruise His heel.   Gen 3:15

It is not only important to understand the patterns of God but also to do His work according to His patterns. When God wants to do something He starts by giving the pattern. So it was for the tabernacle. Jesus is similarly the pattern for the Christian. And so on.

God does not change, so it is for His patterns. It is the nature of God that He cannot compromise in His patterns, principles. His patterns are discovered in His Word. In this book we will discuss some of the patterns recognizable in the nature of God. May God give us the grace to know His patterns, so that we may know Him and understand His ways and become faithful servants of the most high. God works with patterns. The pattern for God's manifestation is Grace, Faith and Obedience.

The mysteries of God are only accessible by those who diligently seek Him.

Secret 3

The ways of God are mysterious

Divine Intelligence

The power and the greatness of God are revealed in creation. To get an idea of the greatness of our God, we can simply look at His creation. The earth is one of about **400 billion planets** that belong to the Milky Way galaxy, one among about **200 billion galaxies**. That means there are around **80 trillion planets**, if each galaxy averages the same number of planets as ours does. Earth is no bigger than a grain of sand on the scale of the universe. However, on earth we can enjoy the beauty and the taste of millions of species of plants and animals, on the ground, in the air, and in the sea. Some are very large and others smaller, very small, that can only be seen with a microscope. In the microscope we can see an entire world that cannot be seen with our natural eyes. In the blood, saliva, everywhere we are surrounded by an invisible world. It is amazing to see the complexity of creation even on a very small scale. Even on the very small scale, we discover structures that are very organized and logical. God reveals Himself as great in the infinitely large and great in the infinitely small.

> *Because what may be known of God is manifest in them, for God has shown it to them. For since the creation of the world His invisible attributes are clearly seen, **being understood** by the things that are made, even His eternal power and Godhead, so that they are without excuse,*   *Rom 1: 19-20*

What a great revelation we have from these scriptures! We can understand God by His creation. By simply looking at creation we can understand how God works.

How does God work?

As a basis for understanding, it is crucial to know that God's intelligence, what we call divine intelligence, is different from man's intelligence. God's operation (ways) is different from man's operations (ways). The solution of God will always be preferred over the solution of men. This is a prerequisite when you try to understand how God works. Because our vision is limited compared to His scope, we are unable to understand the impact of our ways.

> *For my thoughts **are not** your thoughts, neither are your ways my ways, says the LORD. For as the heavens are higher than the earth, so are **my ways higher than your ways**, and my thoughts than your thoughts.* Isa 55:8 -9

God's intelligence is different from man's intelligence; working in different domains. Man's intelligence was given to reign over earth. Man was created to be on earth what God is in heaven. Therefore man is the visible manifestation of the invisible God, created after the image of God.

> *And God said, **Let us make man in our image**, after our likeness: and let **them have dominion** over the fish of the sea, and over the birds of the air, and over the cattle, and over all the earth, and over every creeping thing that creeps on the earth.*
> Gen 1:26

We cannot understand the fullness of what God has created. There are more than one hundred specialties in the medical field, all related to man, to understanding how man functions and providing remedies for his dysfunctions.

Because God's ways are higher than our ways, everything God will do will appear as a miracle to man. Because we do not understand the means by which God acts, His actions to us are miraculous. Everything is easy for Him; He simply speaks it into existence. From God's perspective it is not a miracle, but His mode of action.

Every time we invite God in a situation we must be prepared for a miracle, something we don't understand. It is written:

> ...*the foolishness of God is wiser than men*; and
> *the weakness of God is stronger than men.*   1Co 1:25

Even the foolishness of God is wiser than men. This means every act of God will be greater than men's acts, seen as a miracle by mankind. Actions are simple fruits of thoughts, intelligence. When God does a thing it is always above and beyond man's intelligence. God may act through man, in ways that man can understand, when man serves as God's hands and feet in serving others. However, there are things that only God can do, and when God Himself is doing something, it will always be something men cannot do: it is beyond our understanding. God's ways are different than men's ways.

Paradox

That God's ways are not man's ways leads to what man sees, in his limited logic, as paradoxes. Much in the Bible appears paradoxical. Jewish rabbis understood that God alone understands all, and they understood and taught that mystery and paradox are often signs of the divine nature. (Marvin Wilson, Our Father Abraham: The Jewish Roots of Christian Faith - Eerdmans, 1989)

> *There is a way that seems right to a man, But its end is the way of death.*   *Proverbs 14:12 & 16:25*

Paradoxes such as Jesus's being both fully God and fully human are not possible for human logic to grasp, but must be taken as the Truth of God's nature. Paradoxes abound in Jesus's sayings, such as:

> *"For whoever exalts himself will be humbled, and he who humbles himself will be exalted."*   *Luke 14:11*

> *"And indeed there are last who will be first, and there are first who will be last."*   *Luke 13:30*

> *"Most assuredly, I say to you, unless a grain of wheat falls into the ground and dies, it remains alone; but if it dies, it produces much grain. He who loves his life*

will lose it, and he who hates his life in this world will keep it for eternal life."

John 12:24-25

"If I then, your Lord and Teacher, have washed your feet, you also ought to wash one another's feet."

John 13:14

"You have heard Me say to you, 'I am going away and coming to you.'"

John 14:28

Jesus knew that even His disciples who had spent time with Him could not fully understand all that He wanted to be able to share with them.

"I still have many things to say to you, but you cannot bear them now. When the Spirit of truth comes, he will guide you into all the truth; for he will not speak on his own, but will speak whatever he hears, and he will declare to you the things that are to come.   *John 16:12-13*

Paul also writes of these issues.

Where is the wise? Where is the scribe? Where is the disputer of this age? Has not God made foolish the wisdom of this world? For since, in the wisdom of God, the world through wisdom did not know God, it pleased God through the foolishness of the message preached to save those who believe.

1 Corinthians 1:20-21

Because the foolishness of God is wiser than men, and the weakness of God is stronger than men.

1 Corinthians 1:25

18 Let no one deceive himself. If anyone among you seems to be wise in this age, let him become a fool that he may become wise. 19 For the wisdom of this world is foolishness with God. For it is written, "He catches the wise in their own craftiness"; 20 and again, "The Lord knows the thoughts of the wise, that they are futile."   *1 Corinthians 3:18-20*

And Jesus sums it up, thanking God the Father for the very way that He touches the world in His way, which is paradoxical to mankind.

In that hour Jesus rejoiced in the Spirit and said, "I thank You, Father, Lord of heaven and earth, that You have hidden these things from the wise and prudent and revealed them to babes. Even so, Father, for so it seemed good in your sight."   *Luke 10:21*

The very center of Christian belief, the Resurrection, makes the paradox of God's way very clear, that it is through suffering that we are cleansed and reborn into His life for us.

"He who loves his life will lose it, and he who hates his life in this world will keep it for eternal life."

John 12:25

We seek to end our suffering, but our own growth in God may only come through suffering.

In this book we do not have the pretention to put God in a box. Rather, we identify God's patterns in creation and works. When we identify a pattern in God's creation, it helps us to see His nature, the principles under which He works. When man designs, invents or creates according to God's principles it will always result in a great success. When initiatives follow God's patterns, they will always result in great success.

Everything that we see is a shadow cast by that which we do not see.

- Martin Luther King, Jr.

Secret 4

Life comes from the invisible

Visible and invisible

*For by him were all things created, that are in heaven, and that are in earth, **visible and invisible,** whether they be thrones, or dominions, or principalities, or powers: all things were **created by him, and for him**:*   *Col 1:16*

God created visible things and invisible things. Everything we see comes and lives from what is unseen. What you see comes from what you don't see and lives from what you don't see. Look at nature. The tree you see comes from God you don't see and lives from its roots buried in the ground you don't see. Men and women you see come from God you don't see and a life is sustained by the blood circulating in lungs, heart and vessels you don't see.

> For the **life of the flesh is in the blood**: and I have given it to you upon the altar to make an atonement for your souls: for it is the blood that makes atonement for the soul. *Lev_17:11*

So it goes with all creation: animals, fishes, plants. The very thing that sustains life is always hidden. It is vital to understand this principle. Even man's inventions teach us that. The engine in the car is hidden but if something is wrong with the engine the whole car stops working.

The foundation of the house is hidden, if something is wrong with the foundation the whole building will collapse. My wife and I were looking for a house to buy last year. We saw a great deal, a house that fitted all our criteria at almost half the market price of normal circumstances. As we were looking at the house, in the kitchen we saw a crack in the floor. The foundation was broken. There was no need to look further. Who will buy a house with a broken foundation?

> **If the foundations be destroyed, what can the righteous do?** *Psa 11:3*

Look around, your clock, your phone, planes, computer, tablets, light bulbs, microphones, TV, they are all designed the same. What causes them to work is always hidden. If something is wrong in the hidden, driving parts, the whole thing stops functioning.

The root cause of every problem is invisible

When men and women are sick, they go to the hospital. To diagnose the sickness the doctor will request some tests. A sample of blood will be taken; with the microscope the lab technician will look at the blood to evaluate what cannot be seen with natural eyes. An X-ray test will attempt the same thing; see what cannot be seen with natural eyes. So it is with every problem and trouble you are facing, the root cause is unseen. Men always attempt to solve their issues from a visible perspective while the root cause is always invisible.

David Oyedepo is the Bishop of Winners Chapel that owns the biggest church facility in the world. Months after he launched that facility, the ministry was not growing. He took three days of prayers and fasting and God showed him in a vision, a dark cloud over the church. He prayed until the dark cloud disappeared. That was the break needed, and today he is holding four services each worship day in an auditorium seating seventy thousand.

Marriages are broken from the supernatural; wars start from the invisible world. Sickness, poverty, illness and diseases all start from the invisible world, from what is unseen. The root cause of every problem you or I are facing is from the devil we don't see with our natural eyes. Therefore every fight of your life must be fought in the invisible world.

> *For we wrestle not against flesh and blood, but against principalities, against powers, against the rulers of the darkness of this world, against spiritual wickedness in high places.*   *Eph 6:12*

Therefore, every time you address a problem in the visible world, from what you see, you only address the symptoms, not the root cause.

From inside out: Christian life.

Remember, everything we see is a representation of something we don't see. The life of what we see comes from what we don't see. God spoke life into existence and breathed life into man. (Gen 1-2) Multiplication is done in secret. Our parents conceived us in secret. (Psalm 139:13-

16) Life comes from a secret. Pregnancy is evidence the pregnant woman has done something in secret.

> *...as we look not to the things that are seen but to the things that are unseen. For the things that are seen are transient, but the things that are unseen are eternal.* 2 Cor 4:18

Christian life flows from the invisible

Christianity is the result of the new covenant between men and God. A Christian is a human being with a covenant with God. A covenant is an agreement between two parties based on trust. It differs from a contract. You can be in a contract with a person you don't trust, indeed a written contract is generally done with one not trusted, thus serving as a sign of acceptance of terms between parties. Every party must understand and know in depth the terms and obligations of the contract or covenant that engaged them. So every Christian must know and understand the new covenant, what God's responsibility is and what man's responsibility is. Several times in the Bible a new covenant is mentioned and described in detail, a covenant every Christian should know by heart. It was prophesized by Ezekiel about six hundred years before Christ. There is it written:

"And I will sanctify My great name, which has been profaned among the nations, which you have profaned in their midst; and the nations shall know that I [am] the LORD," says the Lord GOD, "when I am hallowed in you before their eyes. For I will take you from among the nations, gather you out of all countries, and bring you into your own land. Then I will sprinkle clean water on you, and you shall be clean; I will cleanse you from all your filthiness and from all your idols. I will give you a new heart and put a new spirit within you; I will take the heart of stone out of your flesh and give you a heart of flesh. I will put My Spirit within you and cause you to walk in My statutes, and you will keep My judgments and do [them]. Then you shall dwell in the land that I gave to your fathers; you shall be My people, and I will be your God. "I will deliver you from all your uncleannesses. I will call for the grain and multiply it, and bring no famine upon you. And I will multiply the fruit of your trees and the increase of your fields, so that you need never again bear the reproach of famine among the nations. Then you will remember your evil ways and your deeds that [were] not good; and you will loathe yourselves in your own sight, for

your iniquities and your abominations. Not for your sake do I do [this]," says the Lord GOD, "let it be known to you. Be ashamed and confounded for your own ways, O house of Israel! Thus says the Lord GOD: "On the day that I cleanse you from all your iniquities, I will also enable [you] to dwell in the cities, and the ruins shall be rebuilt.   *Eze 36:22-33*

In the book of Hebrews the same covenant is recalled and summarized. There, it is written:

For this [is] the covenant that I will make with the house of Israel after those days, says the LORD: I will put My laws in their mind and write them on their hearts; and I will be their God, and they shall be My people. None of them shall teach his neighbor, and none his brother, saying, 'Know the LORD,' for all shall know Me, from the least of them to the greatest of them. For I will be merciful to their unrighteousness, and their sins and their lawless deeds I will remember no more.   *Heb 8: 10 -12*

What a beautiful covenant, how great is God's part. The question is what is out part is the covenant? Men came to Jesus and asked Him the question:

45

*"What shall we do, that we may work the works of God?" Jesus answered and said to them, "This is the work of God, **that you believe** in Him whom He sent."* Jn 6:28-29

Throughout the Bible it is clear without a shadow of a doubt. The only part that man has to play in the covenant is: FAITH.

When we understand that it is God's part to clean us, to change our heart to cause us to walk in His way, then we can choose to *believe or not* the work of Jesus. The covenant of God has been fulfilled in Christ Jesus.

God changes our inside, our heart, and that causes us to live according to His will. God is Spirit. He works in the spirit realm. He sees from the spirit realm. What we do on the outside is simply a result of what we possess on the inside. A true Christian is a person who has been changed inside, causing him or her to manifest the life of Christ. When we don't possess His Spirit on the inside, we have right to come to the throne of grace and plead with God to play His part. Therefore, prayer for sanctification is abiding in God by faith believing He will transform our heart, causing us to take possession of His divine nature – His Spirit.

A friend of mine, a prayer partner, came to me one day and told me he was very disappointed by his own behavior. He had been fighting with sexual immorality and masturbation for months; he wasn't in peace with what he was doing. He asked me if I knew a hospital where he could be castrated. I fervently discouraged him, telling him that is not his part of the covenant. He simply has to believe what God has already done. So many Christians are discouraged today because they have tried to play God's part in the covenant. They have tried to sanctify themselves. When we don't possess on the inside the life of God we must believe and pray till we possess it on the inside. In his treatise, Fear and Trembling, Kierkegaard discusses the dilemma of Abraham who is called to sacrifice his only son, Isaac. Abraham is held up as the ultimate example of faith (Hebrews 11:8). Kierkegaard calls such examples "knights of faith" and says "On this the knight of faith is just as clear; all that can save him is the absurd; and this he grasps by faith." This is the paradox of the invisible, that which we are required to do. It is absurd, yet we must believe.

Another great number of Christians are falling out from grace because they think they can be made right based on what they do or do not. They judge themselves from the outside, the worldly view. Christianity is from inside out, this is the paradox. This is how Jesus explains it:

You have heard that it was said to those of old, 'You shall not commit adultery. But I say to you that whoever looks at a woman to lust for her has already committed adultery with her in his heart.

Mat 5: 27-28

God who is in the invisible judges from what he sees in the invisible. Before you commit adultery you have done it already in the invisible, in your heart. Jesus came to change the invisible. My faith is based on what I do in the invisible, in the secret of my heart.

Why did Jesus challenge the Pharisees? They were serving at the temple. They were of the lineage of Abraham, Isaac and Jacob; they used the same Scripture He used. What brought the passion that he launched into the "woe to you Pharisees" passage? They were living examples for men; they sacrificed their lives to serve God. But their example was for show. It was not of the invisible, but the visible. This is the answer.

Woe to you, scribes and Pharisees, hypocrites! For you cleanse the outside of the cup and dish, but inside they are full of extortion and self-indulgence. Blind Pharisee, first cleanse the inside of the cup and dish, that the outside of them may be clean also. Blind Pharisee, first cleanse the inside of the cup and dish, that the outside of them may be clean also. Even so, you also outwardly appear righteous to men, but inside you are full of hypocrisy and lawlessness. Mat 23:25-28

Before God you are not sanctified (made holy = acceptable to God) based upon what you do or don't do. God sees your heart, and only a heart that has been washed and cleansed with the Blood of Jesus can be clean before God. It is IMPOSSIBLE for any man to be right before God by himself. We are pure because we have been purified by Him, because we received a new heart from Him and therefore we can do what He requires of us.

Those who heard it said, "Then who can be saved?" But he said, "What is impossible with men is possible with God." Luke 18:26-27

When you place your check point on the inside, you fight victoriously. You are proactive; you win all your battles. When you fight from the outside you fight in defeat. Watch from the invisible. Fight from the invisible. The difference between the old covenant and the new covenant is that the old deals with the visible while the new deals with the invisible.

When God called me into the ministry, I could barely pray for an hour. I knew from the beginning, it was impossible to be effective in God's service with a poor prayer life. Every man of God who has impacted people's lives was first a man of prayer, without exception. A message is void if there is no prayer behind it. I knew my ministry would be useless if my prayer life did not experience a drastic change.

I went to a retreat, knowing it is impossible to pray effectively without a visitation from God. I put aside 21 days to seek God. I was crying out to God day and night: "God I need to pray, I need to be empowered to pray". One night around 10 PM I was crying out to God with great intensity when I felt a deep presence of the Spirit, a supernatural strength to pray, like a river of prayer erupting out of my belly. I prayed until morning. My prayer life was changed forever. It naturally flows from inside out. From that day until today, I have experienced the manifestation of the grace of God in prayer, causing me to pray beyond my imagination. There is not one thing that God requires of us that we can do with our natural strength. Jesus said:

"For without Me you can do nothing."   Jn 15:5

Every request from God is an invitation to come and get it from Him. And He will do it from the inside, where no man can see. Our lives become the testimony of God's visitation. Our role in the covenant is that we believe.

> *"What shall we do, that we may work the works of God?" Jesus answered and said to them, "This is the work of God, **that you believe** in Him whom He sent."* Jn 6:28-29

Jesus is the Son of God because He does God's Will. He always sought His Father's Will.

> *But he would withdraw to desolate places and pray.* Luke 5:16

And His call to us is "Follow me."

And if one overthrows him,

two shall withstand him;

and a threefold cord is not

quickly broken.

-Ecc_4:12

Secret 5

Creation is bipolar

The bipolarity of creation

The atom is a basic unit of matter (generally considered to be anything that has mass and volume) that consists of a dense central nucleus surrounded by a cloud of negatively charged electrons. The basic element which is in all we see is made of negative and positives forces. The stability, cohesion of matter is held by opposite forces that attract.

A magnetic field is created by magnetic poles that cannot exist apart from each other; all magnets have north/south pairs which cannot be separated without creating two magnets each having a north/south pair. Earth itself, and all "the heavenlies" have north and south poles, and magnetic fields.

Therefore we can deduce that the visible world is maintained by opposite forces that attract. All matter is made of positive and negative forces that are attracted to each other.

[1] In Chinese philosophy, "yin and yang", literally meaning "shadow and light", is used to describe how polar opposites or seemingly contrary forces are interconnected and interdependent in the natural world, and how they give rise to each other in turn in relation to each other. Yin and yang are not opposing forces (dualities), but complementary forces, unseen (hidden, feminine) and seen (manifest, masculine), that interact to form a greater whole, as part of a dynamic system. Everything has both yin and yang aspects as light could not be understood if darkness didn't exist, and shadow cannot exist without light. When we read the Bible we discover that every virtue has its complementary element. In his letter to Galatians, Paul notes,

> *For the desires of the flesh are against the Spirit, and the desires of the Spirit are against the flesh, for these are opposed to each other, to keep you from doing the things you want to do.*   *Gal 5:17*

Further, he describes the fruit of the Spirit, the desires we must keep in our soul.

> *But the fruit of the Spirit is: love, joy, peace, long-suffering, kindness, goodness, faith, meekness, self-control; against such things there is no law.*
>
> *Gal 5:22 -23*

One challenge for Christians is to keep the fruit of the spirit at work in their life. Given that everything has its complement, every emotion has its complement; we cannot develop an emotion and ignore its complement. For example we cannot develop love if we don't develop its complement. We cannot develop self-control if we don't develop its complement. It is important to know and understand that complementary is different from opposite. Webster defines *complement* as "something that fills up, completes, or makes perfect," and lists one synonym as "counterpart."

We have been created by God. Everything in us: body soul and spirit. Every feeling and every emotion has been created by God. Sin has opened the door for the misuse of our emotions and feelings. They have been created by God for a purpose, and all that God has created is good. Anger, violence, hatred, fear and other emotions we consider as "bad" have been created by God for a purpose.

Most of us have not been trained to develop and use the "bad" emotions appropriately. For example love can only be developed and maintained by developing the appropriate hatred. These things are mysteries, but are important to know. The first and greatest command is to love God with all our heart, mind, soul, and strength (Mark 12:20). In Paradise, mankind lived in the Presence of God (Gen 3:8) and will live in the Presence of God (Rev 21:3). Anything that separates us from God is termed *sin*. God loves mankind. And His wrath is not against man, but is against sin. He hates anything that separates man from His Presence, because he knows that leads to death. As we grow to love God more and more we come to despise sin, more and more.

> *For the wrath of God is revealed from heaven against all ungodliness and unrighteousness of men, who by their unrighteousness suppress the truth.*
>
> *Rom 1:18*

When we turn our backs on Him, He allows that we reap the consequences of our behavior.

Therefore God gave them up in the lusts of their hearts to impurity, to the dishonoring of their bodies among themselves, because they exchanged the truth about God for a lie and worshipped and served the creature rather than the Creator, who is blessed forever! Amen.   *Rom 1:24-25*

Hatred in the bible

The love of righteousness in the life of Jesus was maintained by the hatred of iniquity.

*You have **loved** righteousness and **hated** iniquity, therefore God, Your God, has anointed You with the oil of gladness above Your fellows.*   *Heb 1:9*

The fear of the Lord is to hate evil. Therefore we cannot fear the LORD if there is no hatred in our heart.

*The fear of the LORD is to **hate** evil: pride, and arrogance, and the evil way, and perverted speech, I hate.*   *Pro 8:13*

The reason we do what should not do is the lack of hatred in our heart. As with God, we must not hate people, but love them. But we must hate the actions that lead away from God.

A sister wanted a promotion at work, and she shared with me, asking me to pray for it. She wanted it so badly. I knew a girl she did not like at all called Maguey (not her real name). I asked her: Would you take a promotion if Maguey were to be your manager? She answered, "I would not. For no money under the sun I would I accept working for Maguey." She wanted a promotion but hated the thought of working for Maguey.

The best way to overcome obsession is by developing hatred against it.

We must hate what God hates and love what He loves.

> *These six Jehovah hates; yea, **seven are hateful to his soul**: a proud look, a lying tongue, and hands that shed innocent blood, a heart that plots wicked plans, feet hurrying to run to evil, a false witness who speaks lies, and he who causes fighting among brothers.*   Pro 6:16-19

> *So guard yourself in your spirit, and do not break faith with the wife of your youth. "**I hate divorce,**" says the LORD God of Israel, "and I hate a man's covering himself with violence as well as with his garment," says the LORD Almighty. So guard yourself in your spirit, and do not break faith.*
>
>   *Mal 2:15-16*

If we pray, asking God to help us to love what He loves, we must also ask Him to help us to hate what He hates. If we confess what we love, we must confess what we hate. If we work on developing love, we must work on developing hatred, hatred of the things that separate mankind from the love of God. Those are two complementary emotions, which go together.

It would take another book to go through anger, violence, hatred, fear, jealousy, sorrow and other emotions we consider as "bad". They all have their place in our life and must be used to complement the "good" emotions.

This is the secret to developing the fruit of the Spirit and developing a character that pleases GOD: Developing the complement emotion.

And if one overthrows him,

two shall withstand him;

and a threefold cord is not

quickly broken.

- Ecc_4:12

Secret 6

Creations are three in one

Observing the triune in creation

By observation, we understand that God and His major creations have been made three in one. God is Father, Son and Holy Spirit. Man is body, soul, and spirit. Time is past, present, and future. The reason is given in the book of Ecclesiastes, chapter four, the twelfth verse.

> *And if one overthrows him, two shall withstand him; and a threefold cord is not quickly broken.   Ecc_4:12*

God is Father, Son, and Holy Spirit and made man after his image. So are many concepts of God.

For there are three that bear record in heaven, the Father, the Word, and the Holy Spirit: and these three are one. And there are three that bear witness in earth, the Spirit, and the water, and the blood: and these three agree in one. 1Jn 5:7-8

Three in one is a pattern of God's creation.

Three in one: Completeness

The number three in the Bible means complete, entire, fullness: divine perfection. Abraham brought three measures of meal for his heavenly guests.

There are three great feasts in the Old Testament.

Israel agrees three times to obey God.

The temple of God is divided into three parts.

Jesus was tempted three times.

There are three levels of temptation, the lust of the flesh, the lust of the eyes, the pride of life.

Three great enemies of men are identified in the Bible: The flesh, the world and the devil.

Jesus spent three days in the grave,

Three apostles witnessed Jesus' transfiguration.

We can go on and on.

To know and enjoy the blessings of God you must know the Father, the Son and the Holy Spirit.

To be complete and fulfilled as a person, it should involve your body, soul and spirit.

To make effective use of the time, you must use the past, the present and the future.

To understand something you must discover its three dimensions. When God does a thing, it is three in one. To enjoy the fullness of any thing we must use it in the three dimensions.

So many promises are written in the Bible but we can only access those when we understand the third dimension. For every concept of God has three dimensions. Prayer has three dimensions, praise has three dimensions, faith has three dimensions, and salvation has three dimensions and so on.

If you don't discover the three dimensions of something you cannot enjoy it to its fullest. If you don't discover the three dimensions of prayer you cannot pray effectively. If you don't discover the three dimensions of worship you cannot worship to its fullness.

To discover the three dimensions of something is essential to understand it and mandatory to enjoy it.

By whom we have received grace and apostleship, for obedience to the faith among all nations, for his name.

- Rom 1:5

Secret 7

Grace faith and obedience is one

Grace, Faith and Obedience are one

God works with patterns. The pattern for God's manifestation is Grace, Faith and Obedience.

Grace

The great confusion about the grace of God comes from the perception we have that the grace of God is the unmerited favor received from God independent of our behavior. We tend to see it as what God has decided to do regardless of what we do. This definition is not wrong but has to be placed in context.

John Bevere defines Grace as: Divine empowerment that enables us to go beyond our natural ability [Extraordinary: A Devotional by John Bevere]. It is true that we do not deserve or merit anything God has done, is doing or will do in our life. We are saved by the grace of God manifested in Christ. Even though the grace of God is unmerited and undeserved, that grace is without effect in our life without faith. What God has done for us is grace, but we access it through faith.

> *For by grace you have been saved through faith, and that not of yourselves; it is the gift of God,*   *Eph 2:8*

Faith

And it is impossible to receive from God without faith.

> *But without faith it is impossible to please Him, for he who comes to God must believe that He is, and that He is a rewarder of those who diligently seek Him. Heb 11:6*

A man went on a vacation with his family in a remote area in Africa. His wife and three children, ages six, four, and two, were riding in a jeep with him. The road was very bad. On the way they had a terrible accident, the car turning over. The parents were instantly killed. The villagers rushed to the accident scene. It was too late. The man and his wife were dead, but the three children were without injury. The villagers adopted the children, who lived with one family in the same house. They had no contact with the outside world. They grew up, sometimes wondering why they were the only ones with white skin in the village, but became accustomed to life in the village. One day a missionary passing by was surprised to see three white teenagers in a village. The missionary returned home and in researching, discovered the children were from a very wealthy family, their parents having left them an inheritance in their will. The missionary returned to the village and related the story. The oldest son who was eighteen said he did not believe the story. The second who was sixteen said, "I know it's true, but I can't make the trip back to the city."

Obedience

The last child who was fourteen said, "I am going back to receive my inheritance." He returned with the missionary, on a very painful and difficult journey. He was eventually successful in collecting his money. The grace of God is useless for us without faith. Faith without obedience (works) is dead.

> For as the body without the spirit is dead, so faith without works is dead also.   Jas 2:26

When we truly believe, it produces in us the works, as the evidence of our faith.

Show me your faith without your works, and I will show you my faith by my works.   *Jas 2:18*

It takes grace, faith, and obedience to receive from God. When you believe God releases His gifts when you obey, you take possession. Obedience establishes on earth what has been released in heaven. Obedience is the gateway that authorizes heaven to invade earth. When I obey, I open a door through which my blessings from heaven come to earth.

When I pray, I am truly requesting divine instruction that will release my answer through my obedience.

Moses prayed to God, and God spoke. God does only one thing, "Speaking" according to evangelist Dr. Michael Murdock. We must actively do something to establish on earth what has been released in heaven. That something is obedience.

"Whatever he asked you to do, do it." Mother Mary knows Jesus is not a wine maker, but she wants you come to Jesus to look for a miracle. He will always ask you to do something, and that something is the answer to the problem. What God will ask you to do may not be logical but always going to be possible. Mike Murdock says "God will not ask you to do the impossible but always the irrational." By doing the irrational you establish your faith.

God will ask you to do the possible, and He will do the impossible.

When God says something we must act accordingly. God may not give you a specific instruction, but when He speaks your actions must be in line with what He says.

When I was in college, the second year, I was failing about 80% of all my classes. I was then a new believer. I needed to pass 100% of my classes. I felt so bad in my spirit, knowing it would be a very bad testimony of the faith I was preaching. I spent some time in prayer presenting the problem to God. After few days God responded, "You will pass the classes." I went back to school. At the end of the year I had failed two classes. In the French system, you must pass each year at the college to advance, receiving your bachelor's degree by passing each year's courses. By failing two courses, I could not go to the third-year level for my bachelor's degree. It was very disturbing for me. I prayed, "God you told me I would pass the classes." After sometime in prayer I realized that I had to believe what God told me. I went out and told all my friends and family that I passed the classes. From time to time I checked for lists on the results board, but the situation remained the same, with two failures. When classes began, I went to third-year classes, but my friends were laughing at me telling me that I had failed and could not take courses with them. When I went to the administration office to pay my tuition with money from my father, the woman in charge told me I could not pay the tuition for the third year because I was still in the second year. I went back with the money, saying to myself I can only pay my tuition in the third year and continued to take third-year classes. One morning, a few weeks later, during my morning devotion, I felt compelled by the Spirit to go and pay my tuition. I went back to the same woman and said, "My name is supposed to be in the third year but apparently you left it on the second year." She asked my name and I told her. She checked on the computer and said. "Why do you students like to aggravate us like this? Here is your name in the third year." I was surprised, even shocked. I asked to see the computer and realized that two of my grades had changed.

A child came to His father and said: Father I need to pay my tuition at school. The father gave him a check and said: Go to school and pay your tuition with this. The grace for this child is having a father who is willing to pay for His tuition. Nevertheless the child must believe that the check he received from his father will allow him to pay the tuition. But until the check is given to the school, the tuition is not paid. If we claim to believe God on something, that faith must produce something in us. That is called obedience.

Grace, Faith and Obedience in Prayer.

If a child that is hungry goes to his father and asks: Daddy I am hungry. The father may say

1-   Go and see your mum or

2-   Go to the refrigerator and get some food or

3-   Take this money, go and buy yourself what you need or

4-   Go in my bedroom; there is a book beside the bed. Open it, and you will find $5 inside. Then open the cupboard. On the left you will see another $5. Then go and buy some food for yourself. Or

5-   Wait right here, I am going to make some food for you; be patient; I will be back.

We could keep going with possible responses. For one request of father has so many options. The instructions the father gives to the child are the true answer to his hunger. By obeying his father's instruction he is actually taking possession of the solution to his hunger.

When we have a problem and come to God through Jesus for a solution, we must first realize that it is by grace that we even know we must pray. It is also by grace that we know we must go to the Father through Jesus. It is even by grace that we can pray. Knowing we must come to Jesus is by the grace of God.

> *"No one can come to Me unless the Father who sent Me draws him; and I will raise him up at the last day."*   *John 6:44*
>
> *"and no one can say that Jesus is Lord except by the Holy Spirit."*   *1Cor 12:3*

When we come to God, before even asking anything of Him, we must first believe that He can respond and will respond. That is faith. But without faith it is impossible to please Him, for he who comes to God must believe that HE IS, and that He is a rewarder of those who diligently seek Him. Heb 11:6. When we know God will do what we are asking according to His Word, then we should also have the right expectation, knowing how God will answer. God often answers with an instruction.

It takes faith to pray, but it may take more faith to accept and receive God's answer to our prayer. The most important thing when we are asking something of God is to listen. It is crucial to pray with a listening ear. The answer of God resides in His Word. For the same situation, for different individuals, Jesus did something different to provide the solution. For some He spoke, for others He used His saliva, and so on. He was simply obeying what His Father told Him to do. "...I do nothing of Myself; but as My Father taught Me,..." John 8:28 When we pray, if we have our own expectations for God's answer we will surely miss His answer. When we pray we must believe and expect God to speak. When God speaks, the answer has been released. By obeying, we take possession of the answer. When we pray our ears must be tuned in, to hear from God. The answer is wrapped in God's Voice. Our obedience to His Voice gives us possession of what He has released for us.

Obedience in the new covenant.

There is huge difference between the old covenant in the Old Testament and the new covenant in the New Testament. In the old covenant God commanded the people of Israel to follow the Law of Moses. In the new covenant, we are under the law of the Spirit. The law of the Spirit is greater, and by fulfilling that law, we naturally accomplish the Law of Moses.

For the law of the Spirit of life in Christ Jesus has made me free from the law of sin and death. Rom 8:2

I say then: Walk in the Spirit, and you shall not fulfill the lust of the flesh. *Gal 5:16*

And do not grieve the Holy Spirit of God, by whom you were sealed for the day of redemption. Eph 4:30

It is very important to know that what God requires of us is to be led by His Spirit within us. When we pray we must be led by the Spirit of God. We must open our hearts to receive from Him the Will of God, the "Rhema" of God. Then we must be sensitive and obedient to His Voice within us. By doing so, we are walking in the center of the Will of God for us, in perfect obedience.

Above all else, guard your heart, for it is the wellspring of life.

-Pro 4:23 NIV

The heart is the center of Christianity

– David Oyedepo

Secret 8

The life of a man comes from his heart

The heart

For a very long time, the heart has been associated with feelings and emotion or simply reduced to a pump. It is only recently that scientists have started thinking more about the heart, when a number of patients who have received heart transplant reported changes in their taste, personalities and even their memories. A Swedish study was published in a medical journal (1) in 2001 exploring the public's feelings and ideas about receiving transplanted organs, to "identify consistent attitude patterns," that is "a specific set of attitudes and motives, that formed a consistent picture that was logical and psychologically meaningful" for people who had received donated organs. In-depth interviews were conducted, and the authors found two different conceptions of the body.

For one group, "the body was easily objectified and conceived as machine-like, and did not represent the self. This machine model paved the way for the understanding that body parts needed to be replaced by spare parts. The other conception meant that a new organ would transfer the donor's qualities, i.e. influence the identity of the recipient with regard to behavior, appearance, and personality."

In addition, Claire Sylvia, a woman who received a heart transplant, published a book (2) with William Novak discussing her feelings that her personality traits changed, to a pattern similar to that of the donor.

This should be a clue that the heart is more than a pump or simply associated with emotions and feelings. However the Bible tells us more about the heart. In Biblical times, the concept of the heart included our concepts of heart and mind.

The heard has desires

Delight yourself also in the LORD; and He shall give you the desires of your heart. *Psa 37:4*

The heart has thoughts

But as for me, this secret has not been revealed to me because I have more wisdom than anyone living, but for our sakes who makes known the interpretation to the king, and that you may know the thoughts of your heart.   *Dan 2:30*

The heart has a memory

Let not mercy and truth forsake you: bind them around your neck; write them upon the tablet of your heart: *Pro 3:3*

The heart meditates (Intelligence)

I call to remembrance my song in the night; I meditate within my heart, and my spirit makes diligent search.   *Ps 77:6*

The heart speaks

Your eyes will see strange things, and your heart will utter perverse things. Pro 23:33

When we come to Christ we receive a new heart and Jesus comes to live in it. We must learn to listen to voice of God in our heart.

And I will give you a new heart, and I will put a new spirit within you. And I will take away the stony heart out of your flesh, and I will give you a heart of flesh. Eze 36:26

In the last decade we have seen the emergence of positive thinking as never before. These religious movements embrace spiritual laws of positive thinking and the law of attraction. That could be summarized by: you are result of your thoughts and **you become what you think**. This is a powerful half-truth, but out of context, it can be very destructive. If we can become everything we decide to think then we don't need God. The reality is we cannot always control our thoughts because thoughts come from the heart.

"For from within, out of the heart of men, proceed evil thoughts" - Jesus Christ," Mark 7:2

When Jesus rose from death, He appeared to His disciples. When they saw Him they were afraid and He said to them:

Why are you troubled? and why do thoughts arise in your hearts? Jesus Christ Luke 24:38

This is a revolutionary truth. For many years, the heart was reduced to its biological functions, to a pump. Here Jesus is telling us all what we think comes from our heart. If we become what we think and what we think comes from our heart therefore our life comes from our heart. The richest and wisest man Solomon new it.

> *Keep your heart with all diligence, for out of it spring*
> *the issues of life. -   Pro   4:23*
> *A sound heart is the life of the flesh: Pro 14:30*

Our life is a reflection of our heart. The state of our heart will communicate thoughts to our mind and will be attracted to our life.

The world therefore is the mirror of men's hearts. Wars, crimes, divorces and all calamities are simply a reflection of men's hearts. The Bible gives the origin of the corruption of the heart. Disobedience is the root cause of the corruption of human heart. We are all born with a corrupt heart, and all need a new heart to function according to God's original plans for our life. The disobedience of Adam has changed our nature by corrupting our heart. The good news is Jesus came to give us a new heart.

> *"Woe to you, scribes and Pharisees, hypocrites! For*
> *you clean the outside of the cup and the plate, but*
> *inside they are full of greed and self-indulgence. You*
> *blind Pharisee! First clean the inside of the cup and*
> *the plate, that the outside also may be clean.*

"Woe to you, scribes and Pharisees, hypocrites! For you are like whitewashed tombs, which outwardly appear beautiful, but within are full of dead people's bones and all uncleanness. So you also outwardly appear righteous to others, but within you are full of hypocrisy and lawlessness. Mat 23:25- 28

Your life may look perfect to men, but God reads our heart. The heart is the place to evaluate our life. What is going on within is what matters. What is the state of your heart? What is the voice of your heart? Have you received a new heart? Are you struggling with the state of your heart? Jesus said:

Blessed are the pure in heart! For they shall see God.
Mat 5:8

We must all receive the free gift of God of a new heart. I received strict education from my father when I was growing up. In high school I tried with all my natural effort to follow and keep the rules in vain. I came to the conclusion that it was impossible to follow the Bible. Even when I was outwardly irreproachable, inwardly I was miserable. Everything I was fighting against was living right in my heart. I was miserable to know what I should do but had no strength to do it. When I invited Jesus into my heart at the age of nineteen, I was surprised to see how what I used to love vanished from my heart. It is not an instant transformation, but a clearly marked path.

The reality of Christianity is a changed heart. When our heartbeat does not correspond to our values, we need to ask God to change our heart. The following simple prayer will help you invite Jesus to come and change your heart:

Dear Lord Jesus. I recognize my heart is corrupt. I believe you died at the cross for me. Come and change my heart. Give me a heart to follow you. Amen

---

What happens in your heart is what matters in heaven.

For He knows the secrets of the heart.   Psa 44:21

We are not born again because we recite a prayer, but when we have the evidence within us that our heart has been changed by God. This is the most important thing that can happen to man. Without a change heart it is impossible to be happy, impossible to live a fulfilled life. When that happens, you know it has happened. The evidence of your new heart will be known by you. You will experience a new joy, happiness and peace that could not be explained otherwise.

Beloved, if our heart does not condemn us, we have confidence before God.   *1 John 3:21*

(1) Social Science & Medicine, 2001 May;52(10):1491-9.

(2)Claire Sylvia and William Novak, 1997, A Change of Heart: A Memoir

What then is time? If no one asks me, I know what it is. If I wish to explain it to him who asks, I do not know.

- Saint Augustine

Secret 9

Past, Present and Future are one

I've heard it said by people whose lives seem to be driven by the clock that "time is the worst invention man ever came up with." Let us be clear that man may have invented the clock, and he may be subjecting himself to the clock as an idol, but GOD, our loving Creator, created time. Man is free to use or misuse GOD'S Creation.

Where is the evidence that time is GOD'S creation? The History of Creation

In the beginning God created the heavens and the earth. The earth was without form, and void; and darkness was on the face of the deep. And the Spirit of

89

God was hovering over the face of the waters. Then God said, Let there be light; and there was light. And God saw the light, that it was good; and God divided the light from the darkness. God called the light Day, and the darkness He called Night. So the evening and the morning were the first day. Genesis 1:1-5

When GOD created light:

- It was good

- It was separate from the darkness

- The darkness was called Night, the light Day

It is interesting to look at the meaning of the Hebrew words, which are so often filled with many nuances. The word for light can not only indicate a light shining, but also enlightenment, as we may also use the words in present day English, "I saw the light." and darkness can also mean either dark, blackness, but also obscure or hidden, as our idiom "he's in the dark."

In the last statement of Genesis 1:5, "So the evening and the morning were the first day," the Hebrew word for evening also can mean covering, and the word for morning can mean uncovering or seeking.

GOD first created light, which is good. The light, which reveals, defined time, Night and Day. Before there was light that reveals, there was only the darkness, obscurity. The evening (the covering) and the morning (the uncovering) were the first day.

Time was created with Light, the revealing. Time was created before Place. Place was created on days two and three. Time and Light allow our understanding, with our experiences within Place (here in this Creation, which for us is the Earth, with the firmament above).

Time is the only part of God's creation to which men are subject. In this world we can change in place but not in time. Our lives have gained some influence on time (in the Biblical age time was defined by walking speed. Today time is more defined by jets and the internet.), but only God has dominion over time. He has given us dominion over the rest of His creation. **Though we consider in our minds past, present and future, we cannot separate the present from the past or the present from the future. Our future is in our present and our past is in our present. When we have the right mindset of our past and a clear vision of our future then we live the present in its fullness. We are now what we have done in our past; we will become what we will do in our present. Present actions determine future destinations. Our past and our future reside in our present. Time is one.**

Past

God can do all things but He will never change our past. Changing the past would be breaking the cycle of time. God uses time to develop us, to help us to learn. What occurred in our past becomes a part of us in the present and in the future. When apostles Stephen, Peter and Paul were seized and were appealing to their captors, each of them would appeal to their captors in the logic that the story of the people of God had begun with Abraham and continued through Isaac and Jacob, and forward. In a beautiful explanation of the importance of faith, (Romans 4), Paul gives examples from Israel's past, including Abraham and David. He also compares Adam, the first man with Jesus. Our past helps us to understand who we are in the present and helps to mold our future. But our past is designed to remain in the past. If we are to enjoy life in the present, we must leave the past in the past. For the One who created time, the past, present and future are one. We dwell only in the present.

How to make use of past failures?

People can be paralyzed by their past. We must learn and grow from our past, as God uses time to develop our character, but we must not become stuck in the past. We have all had failures in our past. These are opportunities to learn and to change. The Bible itself is a guidebook for life, the Word of God, based upon the past. We benefit by listening to the Word of God from the past. We learn from the parables that Jesus tells, because though life was very different in Biblical times (the past), people were not.

> *But Jesus did not commit Himself to them, because He knew all men, and had no need that anyone should testify of man, for He knew what was in man.* John 2:24-25

One of the best examples of teaching about life is the story of the woman *"caught in the very act of adultery."* (John 8:3-11) The crowd is ready to stone her for her sin, which by law is punishable by death. Jesus uses the wisdom of the past to focus the present from the crowd mentality to each individual's heart, saying *"He who is without sin among you, let him throw a stone at her first."* He uses the past to teach first the Pharisees. But the Lord goes further to teach the woman, who has apparently had a sinful past, and is in a life-threatening situation in the present. He uses the moment to teach her how to make her future different. *"When Jesus had raised Himself up and saw no one but the woman, He said to her, 'Woman, where are those accusers of yours? Has no one condemned you?' She said, 'No one, Lord.' And Jesus said to her, 'Neither do I condemn you; go and sin no more.'"* If we don't make good use of our past, learning from it, it will destroy our entire life. The past, the present and the future are one. Each time one fails, he or she has failed to know something from the collective past (the story of God's people in the Bible) or from one's own individual past. Every failure can be traced to ignorance.

My people are destroyed for lack of knowledge:

Hos 4:6

The understanding that when we fail, we really have a failure of understanding of the way that life on this Earth is structured, with the tenets that God has shared with us in His Word and in our past experiences, leads us to investigate to gain knowledge and understand the reason for the failure. Understanding the reason for our failure turns the incident into a positive experience. (See chapter on Understanding) The most painful experiences of life are designed to bring us the best knowledge for the future. At two points in the story, Jesus has stooped to the ground to write in the dirt with his fingers. Why does John include this detail? Could it be that it denotes the passage of time for reflection? Perhaps, in response to the incidents in our lives, the way that we are to learn from them is not to have immediate reactions, but to reflect upon them, including reflection from previous life lessons. We must not turn the page of a painful experience without learning the lesson, but we must learn from the experience and move forward. When Jesus shared the lesson with the woman, He tells her to repent, to turn, to change her direction. We should never allow the pain of the past to consume the present. We must deal with the pain and keep the lessons for the future.

> *My brethren, count it all joy when you fall into various trials.*   *James 1:2*

When we have dealt with the past, forgetting the pain, failures and regrets but keeping the lessons, then we are ready for the future. We must leave the past in the past. Knowing that with whatever we have experienced in the past, we are still alive today, God is able to use the past to fulfill His plan in our lives

> *Brethren, I do not count myself to have apprehended; but one thing [I do], **forgetting those things which are behind** and reaching forward to those things which are ahead, I press toward the goal for the prize of the upward call of God in Christ Jesus. Phil 3:13*

How to use past glory?

We should also never relax in our past accomplishments. Our past exploits are just a glimpse of what God can do in our lives in the future. No matter how great the past, our future must be brighter. As we look to the past we find comfort and faith in what God can achieve. If we have been able to do what we have achieved so far, He is faithful to take it further. He builds on what we have learned from the past.

Present

The present is the moment in which we live, the tick of the clock. Our day by day life is the present. Our present is a result of what we have done with our past. Nevertheless the present must NOT be fed from the past. Feeding our present from our past leads to depression, complacency, or pride. The present must be fed by the future. Happiness and joy can only be sustained by hope, and hope is in our future.

> *Now faith is the substance of things hoped for, the evidence of things not seen. For by it the elders obtained a good testimony. By faith we understand that the worlds were framed by the word of God, so that the things which are seen were not made of things which are visible.* Hebrews 11:1-3

How to make use of your time to the fullest?

We must live our life as we will die tomorrow but plan as if we will never die. We must live today, giving our full potential to everything we are doing today and not let the past compromise today's happiness. Remember the past has passed.

Therefore you also be ready, for the Son of Man is coming at an hour you do not expect. Matthew 24:44

Today is the day of our perfect joy. Today is the day we will live to remember. Today is the day of the best training for our destiny. Today is our happy day. We should let no man take away our happiness. Today is the gift that the Lord gives:

This is the day that the Lord has made; let us rejoice and be glad in it.   Psalm 118:24

But in everything we do we must keep in mind that our present actions must be guided by the vision of our future. We have no future if our present actions are not guided by our future. If our future is not in our present then we have no future.

If our future is not in our present then we have no future.

Our eyes must be on our future, our vision. This is the reason we must spend time in prayer asking God to show us what He has prepared for us.

If someone asked what our future plans were and we said: "I think I am going to be a pastor," the next questions should be how many hours we spend in prayer a day, how much time we spend reading the Bible, or seeking God. Then the questioner will know if we truly believe in our vision. What occupies our day is simply an expression of what we believe for our future. We should not deceive ourselves: what we do with our present time will determine what we become in the future. *"Faith IS the substance of things hoped for."* We will never become what we have not focused on in our mind

Future

Our future is our final destination. It is very important to have a clear vision of the future: where we are going. True success starts here: understanding who we are and where we are going. Our life has no meaning until we find the reason we are living, what we have been created for. Life is beyond eating drinking, going to work, paying bills. We are created for something bigger, better and specific to us each as individuals.

*For we are His workmanship, created in Christ Jesus for good works, which **God prepared beforehand** that we should walk in them. Eph 2:10*

Before we each were created God had prepared good works for us. We must develop them and work in them. We came to earth for a specific reason, a plan by God. If we are unaware of our purpose in creation, it is time to spend time with God to find that purpose. It requires determination and prayer to get to the total conviction. It may take some time, but only God can tell us the reason we were created. When we find it, everything else in our life must be dictated by it. Some call it vision, and some a calling.

Jesus spent forty days in the wilderness with multiple temptations, as we all have temptations. Before this, God gave Jesus a vision.

"And suddenly a voice came from heaven, saying, 'This is My beloved Son, in whom I am well pleased.'" Matthew 3:17 Jesus listened to this vision of His future. If he had listened to the voices of the past, as he was rejected in Nazareth, his ministry would have gone nowhere. *"Is this not the carpenter, the Son of Mary, and brother of James, Joses, Judas, and Simon? And are not His sisters here with us?" So they were offended at Him. But Jesus said to them, 'A prophet is not without honor except in his own country, among his own relatives, and in his own house.' Now He could do no mighty work there, except that He laid His hands on a few sick people and healed them. And He marveled because of their unbelief. Then He went about the villages in a circuit, teaching."* Mark 6:3-6

Nothing must altar the vision of our future

It is very easy to be influenced by our experiences, our background, our past mistakes and failures. We must be able to perceive the plan of God for our life beyond everything, without any outside influences or temptations. Nothing and nobody can speak better than God for us and about us as individuals. Reading the word of God, we discover that God has great plans for us.

For I know the plans I have for you," declares the LORD, plans to prosper you and not to harm you, plans to give you hope and a future.   Jer 29:11

God created us and placed in us everything we need to fulfill His plans for our life. Everything we need to fulfill our call resides within us. If we seek God in prayer through Jesus, He will show us our purpose. It is important to know that we are created for His Glory, to reveal and manifest His Glory on earth. God will never show us something out of this pattern. The Ultimate goal for all of Creation is to glorify God through His Son Jesus.

For a prayer to be effective, the heart, the mind and the mouth must be in accord and fully engaged.

Secret 10

The completeness of prayer

The Completeness of prayer

Without any doubt, far beyond anything else, prayer is the most common practice of all religions and the most important in most of them. However the practice of prayer varies from one religion to another, from one denomination to another. This can only be explained by the conception and definition of prayer in each religion. Some will pray in their heart, others will shout, some others silent and so on. This section of the book is not meant to deal with the different forms of prayer, but to attempt to define prayer in the context of the Bible. What is prayer according the Bible: when can you claim you are praying? An effective prayer is a combination of Word of God, the leadership of the Holy Spirit and the heart of a man. You can only claim you are praying when your heart, your mind and you mouth are all engaged in the prayer.

Prayer

The word prayer was translated from more than five different Hebrew words. Every attempt to interact with divinity, with the spiritual world, was translated by the word prayer. This gives us a vague idea to the meaning of word prayer in the context every time we read it in the bible.

People pray in every religion. What is then the difference between prayers of other religions and the prayers of Christians? The Bible is the foundation of faith of every Christian organization. Christians base their prayers on the Bible. Every prayer therefore must be conformed to the Bible. For example it is written:

> *"For there is one God, and one mediator between God and men, the man Christ Jesus; 1Ti 2:5"*

This is the reason why many Christian's denominations will pray and always finish with "in Jesus's name".

Many Christian denominations use the Bible to base their prayers. What is the difference between other religious prayer and the prayers of the sons of God?

For as many as are led by the Spirit of God, they are the sons of God. Rom 8:14

An effective prayer is based on the Word of God and led by the Holy Spirit. You are truly praying when your heart is engaged on the ground of the Word of God under the leadership of the Holy Spirit.

Likewise the Spirit also helps in our weaknesses. For we do not know what we should pray for as we ought, but the Spirit Himself makes intercession for us with groanings which cannot be uttered. Rom 8:26

Word

The word of God is the foundation for everything. God acts only upon His Word. He does everything by His Word.

In the beginning was the Word, and the Word was with God, and the Word was God. The same was in the beginning with God. All things were made by him; and without him was not anything made that was made.

John 1:1-3

The Word of God is God's language. If we want our prayer to be heard and answered we must find the ground on which we stand to pray in the Bible. If you are praying for healing, you should ask yourself on what ground do I stand to ask or command healing? What in the Bible gives the right to ask for healing? The Bible is the recorded will of God. Jesus taught the disciples to pray *"Thy will be done".*

There is no need that you can have that has not been covered in the Bible. All you need is there. Therefore you must look in the Bible, locate the desired blessing and claim it to God.

> *According as his divine power has given unto us **all things** that pertain unto life and godliness, through the knowledge of him that has called us to glory and virtue*   *2Pe 1:3*

Everything you need has been provided at the cross of Calvary. Locate what belongs to you and claim it in prayers.

When I came to Christ the reality of hell struck my spirit. I wondered how I would feel in heaven if my entire family were to be in hell. As the first believer in my family, I experienced strong rejection. I prayed passionately for the salvation of my family, none of whom were believers, every day. Reading the Bible, I came across a scripture in the book of the Acts of the Apostles:

Believe in the Lord Jesus, and you will be saved—
YOU AND YOUR HOUSEHOLD.   *Act 16:31*

This became the ground on which I was standing when I was praying for my family day and night I was quoting back to God His word. It is written: *"Believe in the Lord Jesus, and you will be saved— YOU AND YOUR HOUSEHOLD."* Act 16:31

My brother, beyond all expectations, gave his life to Christ sixteen months afterwards. Jesus appeared to him in his bedroom twice the same night, after that, he knocked at my door at three AM. "I want to give my life to Jesus," he said. He went down on his knees and surrendered his life to Christ, and he has never been the same. Last year he was voted the most listened-to preacher of the French community in Cameroon.

Then my father followed a very religious path with so many good works. He was trying to please God with his good deeds. One day he called me and my brother and told us a story. He said "while I was sleeping I saw myself leaving my body. I knew I was dying, I wanted to say goodbye to the family but it was too fast, I was gone. I was sure I was going to heaven because I had done so many good things, to my big surprise I find myself on my way to hell. I prayed, "Jesus please I don't want to go to hell." A force brought him back

107

to his room and he realized that if he were to die he would be in hell. Then he asked, "What can I do to be saved?" We told him to repent and receive Jesus. With tears in his eyes, the first time in my life to see my father's tears, he went on his knees, repented of his sins and invited Jesus into his heart.

Then it was my mum's turn. When she realized that the family was turning to follow Christ, she went to see a witch magician to stop me from taking more family members into my religion. She told the story to the witch, and he began some incantations. After some time, he turned to my mum and said, "There is no witch in the world that can touch your child. There is a great light around him. I don't want to take your money for nothing. There is nothing I can do against him." Then she came back home and called me and gave her life to Jesus. She told me the story, and that was the last time she ever went to consult a witch. The entire family, six children and parents, came to Christ one after another with a personal testimony for each of them. God confirmed His word. If you stand in the Word of God in faith, it will always come to pass. God answers His word.

Holy Spirit

With all the knowledge we can have of the Bible, we do not know what to ask in divine order. We see "reality" when only the Holy Spirit sees the truth. Every situation we see is simply a reflection or manifestation of a situation we don't see. We must surrender the leadership of prayer to the Holy Spirit, for He is the only one who knows what is going on behind the scenes.

> *Likewise the Spirit also helped our infirmities:* **for we know not what we should pray for as we ought***: but the Spirit itself makes intercession for us with groaning's which cannot be uttered. Rom_8:26*

Sons of God are led by His Spirit:

> *For as many as are led by the Spirit of God, they are the sons of God.* Rom 8:14

We must keep in mind the Holy Spirit must be the driver of our prayer life, the leader of our entire life. We must know His voice and delight to obey His commands.

In the populated city of Douala in Cameroon some years ago, I was invited to preach to a student crusade. The day before the crusade, on my way home I took a taxi cab not knowing it was a cab of thieves. Few feet away, the driver stopped and two armed men entered in the cab. I asked the driver to drop me, but he sped up the car instead. I stayed, praying in my heart, and the cab took an opposite direction of my destination. The Holy Spirit took control of my prayer immediately. I was praying things I never heard before in a language totally strange to me in a strange loud voice. Then I heard the voice of the Spirit. "Open your Bible, put your money inside and throw it away." It was so clear and loud that I could not doubt. I instantly obeyed. I removed the money I had in my pocket, and as the thieves were looking at me, I opened my Bible and put it in. The window glass was open, so I threw my Bible out. The one beside me, who was watching all my movements, seeing that I threw the money out, opened the door while the cab was still driving and jumped out to look for the money. While he was jumping his clothes hung on the door and were stuck to the car. The car was dragging him on the road. Bystanders saw the drama, and many came out. They were thinking it was an accident. When the driver saw that his partner was hung to the car and being dragged on the road, he stopped the car and they all ran away leaving the car in the middle of the road. When I got out of the car, some feet away I found the Bible with all the money inside. The Holy Spirit's leadership of my prayer gave me a total victory. When the Holy Spirit is leading the prayer, the victory is guaranteed. He knows how and what to pray.

The praying man

Prayer can be defined as talking to God. For two people to communicate they must:

1-   Be willing to talk: Engagement of the heart

2-   Speak the same language: The Word of God

3-   Be connected in some way: The Holy Spirit.

The heart

The heart is the center of Christianity. The work of redemption is related to the heart. "A new heart also will I give you, and a new spirit will I put within you:

> *And I will take away the stony heart out of your flesh, and I will give you a heart of flesh.*
>
> *Eze 36:26"*

This is the place where God deals with man. Jesus comes into a man's life through his heart. God want us to fellowship with him with our heart. God is not moved by the tone of our voice but instead by the engagement of our heart.

A hypocrite in the Biblical context is someone who does not speak according to his heart:

Hypocrites! Well did Isaiah prophesy about you, saying:

> *'These people draw near to Me with their mouth, And honor Me with their lips, but their heart is far from Me.*   *Mat 15:7-8*

When you come to the place of prayer, your brain must read what is happening in the heart. If the heart does not reflect the word of God at that very moment, you must pray for your heart first. Your words are important only when they match the reality of your heart.

The attitude of your heart will determine the altitude of your prayer. Your voice matters on earth when only your heart matters in heaven.

The Flow of an effective prayer

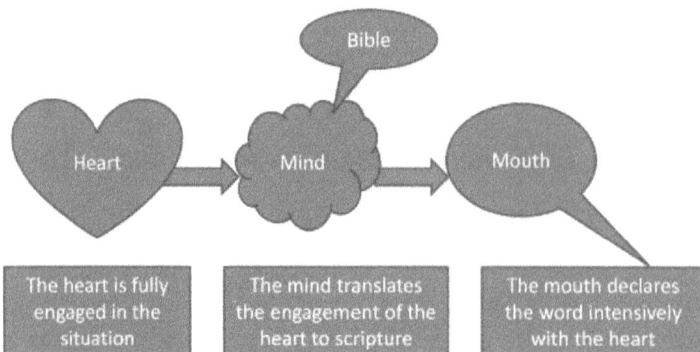

Heart	Mind	Mouth
The heart is fully engaged in the situation	The mind translates the engagement of the heart to scripture	The mouth declares the word intensively with the heart

The mind

Your mind is what translates the feelings and the desires of your heart into a logical structured language then the mouth speaks. It is important to notice that the mind does not drive the prayer. In prayer the mind is subject to the heart. We believe in the heart: when God speaks we must believe. Most of the time God's instruction makes no sense to human intelligence. Moses was in front of the red sea, with Pharaoh behind him, when he cried out to God. God answers:

"Tell the children of Israel to go forward. But lift up your rod, and stretch out your hand over the sea and divide it. And the children of Israel shall go on dry ground through the midst of the sea."   Exo 14:15-16

This makes no sense to human intelligence. If Moses had to think and analyze God's instruction, he would have never obeyed Him.

Jesus told the blind man to go and wash in the pool (John 9:7). This makes no sense to human intelligence to be healed from blindness.

Jesus asks the workers to fill the waterpots with water. (John 2:7) This makes no sense to human intelligence in response to a request for wine.

The foolishness of God is greater than the wisdom of men. 1 Cor 1:25

That is the reason we will never understand God in the beginning, but it will always make plain sense at the end.

The mouth

The declaration of your mouth creates on earth which had been released in heaven. Nothing happens on earth until spoken. The spoken word is the vehicle that brings on earth what was released in heaven. The entire creation was made by the spoken word from God Himself. God said...God said...God said...

And God said, *Let there be light: and there was light.* Gen 1:3 God not only thought of light, he spoke it.

And God said, *Let there be a firmament in the midst of the waters, and let it divide the waters from the waters.* Gen 1:6

And God said, *Let the earth bring forth grass, the herb yielding seed, and the fruit tree yielding fruit after his kind, whose seed is in itself, upon the earth: and it was so.* Gen 1:11

And God said, *Let there be lights in the firmament of the heaven to divide the day from the night; and let them be* *for signs, and for seasons, and for days, and years.* Gen 1:14

God spoke the world into existence. We are created after His own image; we must speak all we want to see. Entire prayers of Jesus and the apostles are recorded in the Bible. They spoke the prayers out.

The intensity of our voice must be proportional to the engagement of the heart.

> *Who in the days of his flesh, when he had offered up prayers and supplications with strong crying and tears unto him that was able to save him from death, and was heard in that he feared; Heb 5:7.*

Many believers are afraid to pray loudly regardless of the prompting of the Spirit. It is important to know that the Spirit can lead us as He wishes. Sometimes we will pray just like Jesus, loudly or softly, depending on the circumstance.

Prayer checkpoint:

Before you pray ask yourself the questions?

1-   Is my heart engaged in this matter?

2-   Is my mind is focused in this matter?

3-   Am I ready to speak out my heart and mind about this?

4-   On which ground of the Word am I standing to pray this prayer?

5-   Is the Holy Spirit leading me in at this moment?

How God answers our prayers?

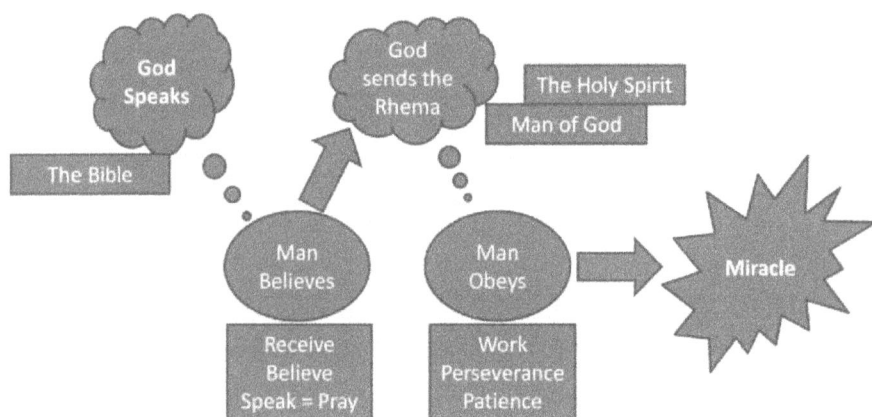

In the example we gave before,

the instructions the father gives to the child are the true answer to his hunger. By obeying his father's instruction he is actually taking possession of the solution to his hunger.

It is very important to know that what God requires of us is to be led by His Spirit within us. When we pray we must be led by the Spirit of God. We must open our hearts to receive from Him the will of God, the "Rhema" of God. Then we must be sensitive and obedient to His voice within us. By doing so, we are walking in the center of the will of God for us, in perfect obedience.

There are only three types of persons in your life, People above you, people around and people under you.

Secret 11

There are only three categories of people in your life

The triune of relations

There are only three types of person in your life, People above you, people around and people under you. You must identify and position every person around you. You success depend on it. A worker who ignores the position of his manager will soon be fired. A citizen who ignores the position of an officer may find himself in jail. Where ever you are and whatever you do, you have three types of people around you. Identify them and position them in your mind and spirit.

Authority

A person in authority over you is a person from whom you receive command, directions, and orders. A person you must obey. Your manager at work, your parents in the house, your pastor at church, your teacher at school, your coach in sport, your mentor in business, the policemen in the street and so on. Those are authority over you in their respective field.

Your manager may be your friend; he may ask your opinion and may even play with you. But never forget he stays in charge and therefore has the final say.

Your parents may play with you, ask your opinion, joke, and dance with you but never forget they are your parents, in authority over you, and they have a final say. Your ears must be inclined to receive from them the wisdom to guide you. Your success is wrapped in your abilities to follow what they tell you, to serve those in authority over you. Sometime it's very difficult to follow 'wrong' or 'bad' instructions. Submission is a principle, a law for ascension. Nothing can justify an insubordination. There is no good way to do a bad thing. Good is good and evil is evil. When it is difficult to follow instructions you must pray both for yourself and the person in charge. Your emotions are not to be involved when it comes to your relation with your authority. What you feel is not relevant when it comes to your duty. When you accept somebody as an authority over you, you must play your role by being submissive to him.

Husband > Wife relation

It is crucial for every husband to understand his role and responsibilities as husband. As a husband you are the priest of your family establish by God to lead the family in the perfect will of God. This role must be understood by the entire household. As the authority you are responsible to teach and empower the household to get to the perfect will of God at the family level and individual level.

This role as been perverted in this generation, many husbands have misunderstood therefore abused their role and operated as dictator instead of lovely leader. As a result of that we have seen the rising of non-submissive wife who refuses to accept the beautiful position of wife.

The authoritative position of the husband is a great responsibility. He is commanded by God to love his wife as Christ loves the church and for whom He gave His life. When the husband truly loves his wife, he is positioned to receive directions from God to bless the family. He is responsible to implement God's plans in the family. He must take time in prayer to receive from God. His authority can only be performed when he is well positioned with God. When he receives from God he becomes responsible to implement God's plans. He must place the will of God above everything: the desires of his wife, children and circumstances.

Many families have been destroyed when the man fails to take his position and allow the family to be led by the wife. When a man does not understand his position and is not ready to carry his responsibilities, he is not qualified to receive directions from God about his family.

Many men today does not take time to seek God for directions, many are afraid to take a position in God's will. Many simply delegate the leadership to the wife. This explains the statistics: One Christian couple out two ends up divorcing.

When God gives us authority, He expects us to use it. We cannot run away from it. If you are not ready to carry your role of leadership in the family as a man, don't get married. It is your responsibility to educate the entire family on it. You are the authority and you must exercise your authority. This does not mean ruling over your wife but simply serving her, empowering her to do the will of God uncompromisingly. You must learn to say a lovely NO to your wife when you know where God is taking you. It is commonly said that any animal with two heads is a monster. You are the only head of the family.

Manager > Employee relation

I personally believe this level of relation is better understood by the majority especially in America. There are two majors philosophies involved here; the kingship and the leadership. The leadership role is well practiced in America while kingship is still practiced in most other countries.

A company I was working for, sent me to Africa to install a management service center, I had to hire and train about twenty support agents. After few days of training, I decided to take my team to lunch. During lunch I tried to be as friendly as possible with everybody, practicing American leadership style. After lunch we went back to class. I started noticing a great change. The phone of one agent rang while I was teaching, she picked it up and started a phone conversation in class, I was horrified. Nobody was attentive anymore. The next day 30 minutes after 9:00AM no one was in class. The class starts at nine. Very few have done their personal work. I realized that my friendly move was very bad. I spent about 30 minutes to share the difference between kingship and leadership. I and told them I will fire half of them by the end of the training if nothing changes. After that, everything came back to normal. Because you have a friendly manager, does not make of him your friend.

The manger is empowered by the company to empower you to bring expected results. A good manager must understand what philosophy fits the best his team: Kingship, leadership or a combination of both.

Friendship

Friendship is the principle that governs your relation with your peer. This is the place to be you. This is the ground where your emotions have the right to be involved. Your relationship is governed by your emotions. You share you joy and pains with your friends. You say what you think, what you want, what you love. You speak your heart with your friend. No one is leading. Together we are facing and enjoying life. If you intend to keep someone as a friend you must tell him/her what you feel. If you are afraid to lose a friend by telling him the truth, you have already lost him/her as friend. You must tell him/her when you are offended. You must tell him/her the truth of your heart. Here is some good advice from Solomon:

A man of many companions may come to ruin, but there is a friend who sticks closer than a brother.
Pro 18:24 NIV

Wounds from a sincere friend are better than many kisses from an enemy.
Pro 27:6 NLT

Relation diagram

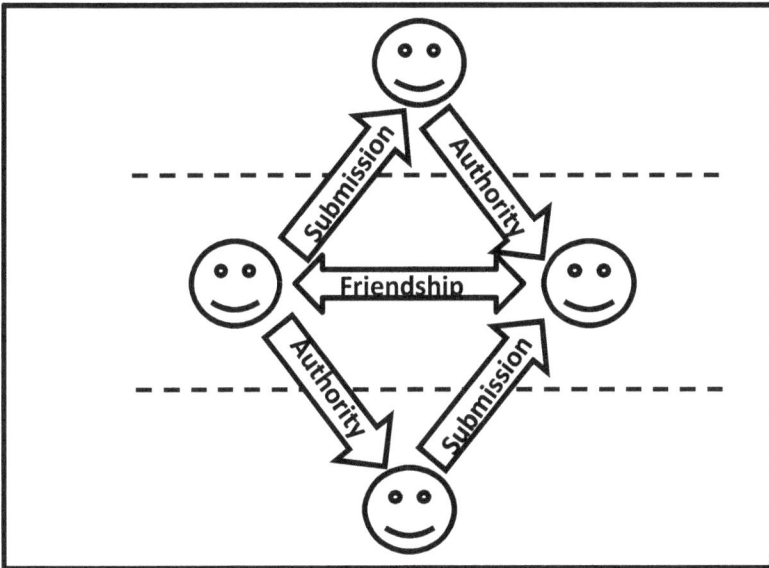

Male and Female He Created Them

Understanding the role and position of each is the key for blooming.

None of us involved in writing this book is putting himself or herself up as the guiding light, the example. Each of us has had struggles in relationships. Each of us has failed. We have each paid the price of broken marriage and divorce. Much effort has gone into healing a marriage that is not healthy, efforts through counseling and praying and painful, determined work. We are fallible, just as the reader is. We know the difficulties and the pain, the times of blaming the other, and the times of a good long look in the mirror. Our thoughts on relationship, shared here, have been led by the Triune God: Father, Son, and Holy Spirit, as He comes to us when we have hit rock bottom. Above all, the insight we have gained is that Christ must be at the center of all we do. And it was a hard lesson to learn. And many people are like unto us, stiff-necked and wanting to do things their own way. We may not be able to prevent your hitting rock bottom. But we can share with you the Way, the Truth and the Life, who will, as you abide in Him, serve as a foundation for building an entirely new life.

He drew me up from the pit of destruction, out of the miry bog, and set my feet upon a rock, making my steps secure. *- Psalm 40:2*

Have faith... Believe in what you feel is impossible... The person you have been can be born again in this life. And it is an amazing transformation, from caterpillar to butterfly. He gives wings...

Jesus answered, "Truly, truly, I say to you, unless one is born of water and the Spirit, he cannot enter the kingdom of God. That which is born of the flesh is flesh, and that which is born of the Spirit is spirit. Do not marvel that I said to you, 'You must be born again.' The wind blows where it wishes, and you hear its sound, but you do not know where it comes from or where it goes. So it is with everyone who is born of the Spirit."

- John 3:5-8

Far be it from us to state that we understand all about God and all His motives. And far be it from us to get into grand debates with people who have made the Bible and Biblical languages their life's work. But we see some themes in the stories in Scripture about men and women that seem to us to be another of those patterns of God, patterns of the nature of Creation. And those we set about to share here. Undoubtedly there will be those whose beliefs are challenged by what we share. That is expected because there is great polarization in today's world between those who believe one way or the other about the sexes and their roles.

We believe it is wise first to state some clear themes in Scripture that apply to all persons, no matter the sex. And the first is that we are created by a loving God. (Gen 1:27, 1 John 4:16) And second is that we can see that He is a loving God by the nature of the Creation around us. (Psalm 19:1-4) And mankind is created by God in His own image. (Gen 1:27) It is therefore in our nature also to be loving.

1 John 4:16

Further, there are patterns or themes, understandings about the nature of creation, that have been handed to us in Scripture as "commands," not because God wants to push us around or because He wants to see us fail. These understandings about the nature of creation are shared with us as "life rules" because He knows the nature of how His creation works, and that if we follow these guides, life will generally be better for us. And if we don't, life will generally be more difficult for us. So, what are these guides? We mostly know them as "The Ten Commandments." but Jesus distilled the essence of these guides into two: (Mat 22:36-40) *"Teacher, which is the great commandment in the Law?" And he said to him, "You shall love the Lord your God with all your heart and with all your soul and with all your mind. This is the great and first commandment. And a second is like it: You shall love your neighbor who is like unto yourself. On these two commandments depend all the Law and the Prophets."*

And He later even clarified that: (John 13:34) *"A new commandment I give to you, that you love one another: just as I have loved you, you also are to love one another."* These life guidelines apply to us all, male and female. And how did He love us? Sacrificially. (John 13:14-17, John 15:13, 2 Cor 13:4) Thus, He expects us to put the other before ourselves.

Scripture is also replete with passages about how God despises haughtiness and pride and loves humility and contrition. (Isa 57:14-15, Isa 66:1-2, 2 Sam 22:28, 2 Chr 7:14-15, Psa 18:27-28, Psa 25:9, Psa 147:6, Psa 149:4, Pro 3:34, Pro 11:2, Zep 2:3, and more)

> *"He has told you, O man, what is good; and what does the Lord require of you but to do justice, and to*

love kindness, and to walk humbly with your God?"

-Micah 6:8

"The sacrifices of God are a broken spirit; a broken and contrite heart, O God, you will not despise."

-Psa 51:17

"Humble yourselves before the Lord, and he will exalt you."   *-Jam 4:10*

Whether male or female, these are expectations of our loving Father. And these foundational expectations we must keep in mind as we try to sort out the issue of male and female relations.

Let us then return to Genesis, "In the beginning..." to sort out some of what we hope to show as themes or patterns.

24 And God said, "Let the earth bring forth living creatures according to their kinds—livestock and creeping things and beasts of the earth according to their kinds." And it was so. 25 And God made the beasts of the earth according to their kinds and the livestock according to their kinds, and everything that creeps on the ground according to its kind. And God saw that it was good. 26 Then God said, "Let us make man in our image, after our likeness. And let them have dominion over the fish of the sea and over the birds of the heavens and over the livestock and over all the earth and over every creeping thing that creeps on the earth." 27 So God created man in his own image, in the image of God he

*created him; male and female he created them. 28 And God
blessed them. And God said to them, "Be fruitful and multiply
and fill the earth and subdue it and have dominion over the
fish of the sea and over the birds of the heavens and over
every living thing that moves on the earth." 29 And God said,
"Behold, I have given you every plant yielding seed that is on
the face of all the earth, and every tree with seed in its fruit.
You shall have them for food. 30 And to every beast of the
earth and to every bird of the heavens and to everything that
creeps on the earth, everything that has the breath of life, I
have given every green plant for food." And it was so. 31 And
God saw everything that he had made, and behold, it was
very good. And there was evening and there was morning,
the sixth day.*   *-   Genesis
1:24-31*

Condensation: God created beasts, after what He had
previously created, and saw that it was good. And then He
said, "Let us make man in our image, after our likeness.
And let them have dominion." "So God created man in his
own image, in the image of God he created him; male and
female he created them." Both male and female are in His
image, after His likeness. God has in His nature both the
likeness of man and of woman.

And He gives them tasks to do, knowing that as He feels
fulfilled in doing this task of creation (It was very good), so
also would mankind made in His likeness, feel fulfilled in

doing tasks, doing them well. (see the Parable of the Talents, Mat 25:14-30 - e.g. *21 His master said to him, 'Well done, good and faithful servant. You have been faithful over a little; I will set you over much. Enter into the joy of your master.'*) The Joy of the Master is in being faithful in what we have been given to do.

What are the tasks we are given?

"Be fruitful and multiply and fill the earth" - we are to procreate. And we are to subdue the earth and have dominion over it. To help understand this part of our "assigned tasks" better, we turn to the second story of creation, in chapter 2 of Genesis. Genesis 2:7-10

The Creation of Man and Woman

7 then the Lord God formed the man of dust from the ground and breathed into his nostrils the breath of life, and the man became a living creature. 8 And the Lord God planted a garden in Eden, in the east, and there he put the man whom he had formed. 9 And out of the ground the Lord God made to spring up every tree that is pleasant to the sight and good for food. The tree of life was in the midst of the garden, and the tree of the knowledge of good and evil. 10 A river flowed out of Eden to water the garden, and there it divided and became four rivers. Eden in Hebrew means pleasure. The word for river comes from a root word meaning, to flow, to stream, to light. The four rivers are Pishon, meaning increase, Gihon meaning bursting forth, Hiddekel (the Tigris), meaning rapid, and the Euphrates, meaning fruitfulness. Begin to get a picture of what it was like? And in verse 5, note, the comment *"no man to work the ground."*

More about the tasks we were given... Genesis 2:15-17 *The Lord God took the man and put him in the garden of Eden to work it and keep it. And the Lord God commanded the man, saying, "You may surely eat of every tree of the garden, but of the tree of the knowledge of good and evil you shall not eat, for in the day that you eat of it you shall surely die."*

We were put in the midst of God's bountiful creation *"to work it and keep it."* And we've already noted that in Chapter One, we've been given dominion over it all. And in addition we now have been given a clear-cut task to obey our Creator: a limit. He gives all, amazing bounty, in His great love for us. And He also gives us a limit, which is also an expression of His great love for us. He knows us - He is our Creator. He loves us so much that He gives us freedom to choose, but He asks that we trust Him enough to know that when He (in His all-knowing state - Psa 139:13, Jer 1:5,

John 2:24-25) gives us limits or guidelines, it is done out of love, for our good.

So, now have three tasks, to procreate, to work the earth of creation, and to obey the guidelines that He gives us. (Deut 13:4, John 15:14 *"You are my friends if you do what I command you."* John 15:17, 1 John 5:2)

And God was well aware that man alone could not accomplish these tasks. Back to Genesis 2:18-25 *Then the Lord God said, "It is not good that the man should be alone; I will make him a helper fit for him." Now out of the ground the Lord God had formed every beast of the field and every bird of the heavens and brought them to the man to see what he would call them. And whatever the man called every living creature, that was its name. The man gave names to all livestock and to the birds of the heavens and to every beast of the field. But for Adam there was not found a helper fit for him. So the Lord God caused a deep sleep to fall upon the man, and while he slept took one of his ribs and closed up its place with flesh. And the rib that the Lord God had taken from the man he made into a woman and brought her to the man. Then the man said,*

"This at last is bone of my bones and flesh of my flesh; she shall be called Woman, because she was taken out

of Man. Therefore a man shall leave his father and his mother and hold fast to his wife, and they shall become one flesh. And the man and his wife were both naked and were not ashamed. "

A lot of controversy has been stirred up in recent years about how to translate those last two Hebrew words in verse 18, "ezer neged." And we're not likely to settle that argument here. We think there are a number of hints in the context that are helpful. But we are not theologians or linguists, just folks who try to listen to the Spirit as He guides us through the Word. One clue to us is that the word most frequently translated as "rib" is most frequently translated elsewhere in scripture as meaning "side." So one could think of woman being formed from the side of man, and to be beside him in his assigned tasks. There is also the statement by Adam that Eve is "bone of my bones and flesh of my flesh," which sounds to us pretty much as oneness, and indeed as the next verse says man shall hold fast to his wife and they shall become one flesh. So, in the hopes of getting you to read further, at this point we are going to come down in the middle of this controversy simply saying that this passage means a "partner suitable for the tasks that man has been given." Male and female He created them, in His likeness. They were to work together, as those having dominion over this bountiful creation to accomplish those three tasks. In order to accomplish those three tasks, they had to be male and female.

Well, OK, they didn't HAVE to be... God is perfectly capable of creating anything He desires. He has created many plants and animals that embody both male and female sexual organs. But there are other aspects of God, that would make that creation not fit His plan for man: *"Let us make man in our image, after our likeness."* (Gen 1:26) First, God's nature, as the Trinity, is one of relationship. And secondly, God is a lover of beauty. He has created abundance and diversity, the earth, the heavens, plants and animals, in great beauty for us to have dominion over. These things are obvious. (see Psa 8:1-4, Rom 1:19-20) And it is only after He created man and woman that He said, *"It is very good."* And if He first created man, and then from man's side created woman, she is the culmination of creation. God's crowning glory. And the crown of man (Pro 12:4) And after this, God rested. It was very good... Recall Mat 25:21 *"Enter into the joy of your master."*

Three tasks, to be done with joy, in Eden (pleasure), without shame.

A brief pause before we get to what we all know "lovingly" as The Fall... word or two to introduce the serpent. We don't know all we would like to know about creation and about how long those "days" really were. We do know this, from Scripture - 2 Peter 3:8 *"But do not overlook this one fact, beloved, that with the Lord one day is as a thousand years, and a thousand years as one day."* We know that at some time before, Lucifer, who was the previous crown of creation (Day Star, son of the morning -see Isa 14:12-17) became filled with pride and tried to exalt his throne above the stars of God and said, *"I will be like the most high."* And we know that after he was brought down (Rev 12:7-9), he roams about on the earth (Job 1:7), and he prowls around looking for someone to devour (1 Pet 5:8). And he continues to fight against mankind (Rev 12:13-17), but we know in the end, he loses (Rev 20:10). But he does not go down easily.

We don't know how long Adam was kicking around in Eden without Eve. Could be a thousand years, could be a thousand millennia. It was long enough for God to see it was not good for man to be alone. And thus He created the crown of creation, the beauty of a suitable partner for Adam. We don't know why Satan, the serpent, the dragon, Lucifer, chose to wait to approach mankind by way of Eve rather than coming earlier to Adam. But we have seen his prideful nature from the Scripture noted above, and we can therefore reasonably surmise that the former crown of creation was envious of the new crown of creation. And so he came in his deceitful way. Telling lies that are truthful enough to make them believable (John 8:44, Acts 13:10, Psa 120:2, Pro 31:30).

Gen 3 - The Fall

1 Now the serpent was more crafty than any other beast of the field that the Lord God had made. He said to the woman, "Did God actually say, 'You shall not eat of any tree in the garden'?" 2 And the woman said to the serpent, "We may eat of the fruit of the trees in the garden, 3 but God said, 'You shall not eat of the fruit of the tree that is in the midst of the garden, neither shall you touch it, lest you die. '" 4 But the serpent said to the woman, "You will not surely die. 5 For God knows that when you eat of it your eyes will be opened, and you will be like God, knowing good and evil." 6 So when the woman saw that the tree was good for food, and that it was a delight to the eyes, and that the tree was to be desired to make one wise, she took of its fruit and ate, and she also gave some to her husband who was with her, and he ate. 7 Then the eyes of both were opened, and they knew that they were naked. And they sewed fig leaves together and made themselves loincloths.

8 And they heard the sound of the Lord God walking in the garden in the cool of the day, and the man and his wife hid themselves from the presence of the Lord God among the trees of the garden. 9 But the Lord God called to the man and said to him, "Where are you?" 10 And he said, "I heard the sound of you in the garden, and I was afraid, because I was naked, and I hid myself." 11 He said, "Who told you that you were naked? Have you eaten of the tree of which I commanded you not to eat?" 12 The man said, "The woman whom you gave to be with me, she gave me fruit of the tree, and I ate." 13 Then the Lord God said to the woman, "What is this that you have done?" The woman said, "The serpent deceived me, and I ate."

Remember, we had three tasks - to obey, to procreate, and to work the earth as our dominion. Before we get to the obvious natural consequences of what followed from the disobedience, we might mention some of the less obvious consequences... SHAME, the awareness of having done wrong... And BLAME, the prideful desire not to take responsibility for our own actions. In the Garden they had been sustained by the life flowing from the Living Water (John 4:10, 7:38) until they sinned (stepped away from God) and they hid themselves (separate from the Presence of God) into darkness, out of the Light (John 8:12, 1 John

1:7). In the darkness, away from the Light, they began to focus even more and more on self (pride is a self-focusing cycle that triggers our not-always-healthy feelings of self-preservation - lies beget more lies - "It wasn't me!" - we can see it in our children).

> *14 The Lord God said to the serpent, "Because you have done this, cursed are you above all livestock and above all beasts of the field; on your belly you shall go, and dust you shall eat all the days of your life. 15 I will put enmity between you and the woman, and between your offspring and her offspring; he shall bruise your head, and you shall bruise his heel."*

Note more support that this was really about Satan purposely choosing the woman as his target, as his rival. This is also noted in Revelation (12:1-4, 12:13, 12:17). Part of Satan's curse is to be at war with woman's offspring, and he in a position to cause pain in our lives but not to claim victory. Whereas all we have to do is resist him and he will flee (Jam 4:7). Perhaps Satan knew that mankind's purpose of fulfilling the three tasks: obeying (trusting) God, procreating, and having dominion had no chance of success when there was just Adam. He was not threatened. But when he saw that God recognized that for Adam alone, things were not good in terms of man's being able to fulfill his role, and God created the missing piece, the pinnacle of creation, which was not only the miracle of Eve, but the miracle of relationship, then he knew (he is wily) that there was a chance of success. And it became his goal to thwart that success in mankind's tasks: to trust God, to procreate, and to work the earth. And see how he immediately went for that first commandment (love the Lord with all your heart... the trusting God part) *"Did God actually say?"* And he brings pride right in with that little questioning of God: *"For God knows that when you eat of it your eyes will be opened, and you will be like God, knowing good and evil."* And when he had planted the pride with the half-truth, Eve lost the trust in God, which put her in Lucifer's place of exalting oneself above God. In her freedom to choose, she chose unwisely. We all do. And it is in our nature here to blame Eve. Adam did, and many of us still do. John's Gospel has a great parable about a woman caught in the very act of adultery (John 8:3-11), which addresses this blame concept well. In His Mercy, He reminds us that it is the one among us who is without sin who should cast the first stone. Jesus does not condemn the woman, but reminds her to turn back to God's way.

Now we continue with the Genesis 3 narrative.

16 To the woman he said, "I will surely multiply your pain in childbearing; in pain you shall bring forth children. Your desire shall be for your husband, and he shall rule over you."

We should go into depth about how this occurred as the natural consequence of the actions taken and the nature of our role in God's creation. Remember the three-fold pattern of our role, and note that as the trusting God part of the triune is broken, the result is a break in the other parts... Here the procreation and relationship necessary to bring about the work of the earth, leading to mankind's dominion, is broken. There is a break in the sexual role leading to procreation. And there is a break in the relationship between the two "suitable partners" who are to work the earth together. And remember how the sum of the law and the prophets is to love God and love neighbor. With the breaking of the love God portion, the love of neighbor is also lost.

> *Gen 3:17 And to Adam he said, "Because you have listened to the voice of your wife and have eaten of the tree of which I commanded you, 'You shall not eat of it,' cursed is the ground because of you; in pain you shall eat of it all the days of your life; 18 thorns and thistles it shall bring forth for you; and you shall eat the plants of the field. 19 By the sweat of your face you shall eat bread, till you return to the ground, for*

out of it you were taken; for you are dust, and to dust you shall return."

And, going into depth about how this occurred as the natural consequence of the actions taken and the nature of our role in God's creation, we note that God points out to Adam that there was a choice made here, a selfish and prideful choice to listen to a person before listening to Him. The trust is broken, another has been placed higher than God, and as a result also that role of working the earth will no longer be easy. There will not be the natural connection to the river of Living Water, but man's efforts will be more difficult, thwarted by thorns and thistles. Relationship, the God way of allowing the free-flow of working the earth, leading to man's dominion, is now broken. Now we must seek relationship with God... He is still there, walking in paradise in the mist of the evening, but we do not have that daily walk with Him in the Garden unless we seek it. We must work for it, and there are many potential hurdles to our entering the Kingdom: Satan laying down his traps, tribulations and persecutions in this life, the cares of the world, the deceitfulness of riches, and the desires for other things (see the parable of the Sower and Jesus's explanation of the parable Mark 4:2-20).

Creation works the way it works. It fits with the nature of God. God tells us in Scripture pretty clearly what His nature is like. And He tells us, again pretty clearly, that *"the ones who hear the word and accept it"* are the ones who *"bear fruit, thirtyfold and sixtyfold and a hundredfold."* (Mark 4:20) The message is the same throughout the entire Bible.

> *Gen 3:20 The man called his wife's name Eve, because she was the mother of all living. 21 And the Lord God made for Adam and for his wife garments of skins and clothed them. 22 Then the Lord God said, "Behold, the man has become like one of us in KNOWING good and evil. Now, lest he reach out his hand and take also of the tree of life and eat, and live forever—" 23 therefore the Lord God sent him out from the garden of Eden to work the ground from which he was taken. 24 He drove out the man, and at the east of the garden of Eden he placed the cherubim and a flaming sword that turned every way to guard the way to the tree of life.*

An important point here about the verb "to know" - it is the Hebrew word yada' - and it is an action verb. It has a very broad range of possible meanings, but it has a great depth - it may mean to know, not perceive, to understand, and as is frequently used in the Bible, as in Gen 4:1 *Now Adam knew (yada') Eve his wife, and she conceived and bore Cain, saying, "I have gotten a man with the help of the Lord."*

So, God was aware that mankind had come to experience not only good, as it had been in Eden, but now had experienced evil: deceit, lies, shame, blame. And thus He mercifully shut out the possibility that, in that state of knowing both good and evil, man's time would be unlimited. If man partook of the tree of life in his state of living both good and evil, he would live eternally in that state. He thus mercifully limited our time in the flesh, knowing evil, that we might have the opportunity to live forever in the state of knowing only good (the Kingdom of God, the New Jerusalem, Heaven). He gives us that opportunity if we will again come to Him. Just as in James 4:7-10, we are told, *"Resist the devil, and he will flee from you."*, James 4:8 shows how we can attain the goal of the Kingdom of Heaven, east of Eden, *"Draw near to God, and he will draw near to you. Cleanse your hands, you sinners, and purify your hearts, you double-minded. 9 Be wretched and mourn and weep. Let your laughter be turned to mourning and your joy to gloom. 10 Humble yourselves before the Lord, and he will exalt you."* If we seek all the wealth and happiness of this world, we seek the prideful way of the serpent. If we, instead, choose humility, we will be exalted.

Now we are at a point of looking at the roles of the sexes, male and female, and we need to reiterate that we are all created in God's image and that God loves us. We need to reiterate that God desires of us humility, that we trust Him. And that He despises pride and haughtiness: that brought about the fall from greatness of Lucifer and it broke the relationship of man and woman with God and the relationship of the sexes, one with the other. Rather than the natural flow of the suitable partners working together to procreate and work the earth, we see discord in the work, discord in the procreation, and discord in the relationship. Life is not easy. But as we have looked to Scripture to help us understand all the other patterns we have shared, so we will look to Scripture to help us understand the male and female roles in our world, now east of Eden.

And we will begin with a very clear indication of the current "fallen" state, which is the all-too-well-known statement, "It's a man's world." It's a famous quotation; no one knows exactly where it originated; it has been popularized by a James Brown song and a quotation by Marilyn Monroe; it has been the topic of many discussions in the women's movement and the topic of many jokes by both men and women. And the very statement already assumes the fallen state that we are in. There is already division... there is a separation of the God-created relationship, whereby man and woman are joined together as one flesh. There is already a state of "otherness;" pride is there with its shame and blame. We have already seen that aloneness for man was "not good," and that in the creation of relationship, it was "very good." Does it really, really matter that man came first, then woman? It probably does matter, in that this is the way that God designed it, but is His purpose in that action clear to us? No. Some things we have to take on faith. After all, that is what He asks us, to trust Him, to follow Him. We cannot understand all His ways (Isa 55:8, Psa 25:4, 119:15). As a popular statement goes, "It is what it is." (Reflects an old Biblical saying, "I am who I am.")

Again, we will not convince you as reader to change your belief about that statement, "It's a man's world." But we can work with that statement, that understanding, wherever it is that you come down on your beliefs. It does reflect mankind's fallen state of tension between the sexes. It is what it is. But what does that have to do with you as a male or female in understanding your role here on God's earth? I remind you that there are many expectations of us all as human beings, which is where we started. I love that scripture in Micah:

> "He has told you, O man, what is good; and what does the Lord require of you but to do justice, and to love kindness, and to walk humbly with your God?" (Micah 6:8)

Here the prophet is not speaking to man as male but man as male and female. Many are the expectations, but if we look at our tasks, He did create male and female separately; we are not the same (we thank God for that!!). Males have certain attributes that led to the consequences noted in Genesis 3 for Adam. And females have certain attributes that led to the consequences noted for Eve.

Perhaps as we explore those consequences, we can learn more about our individual roles. And then we can look at some scriptural examples of what it means to be a man in God's eyes and what it means to be a woman in God's eyes. But one more step back to note that, just as we cannot understand all of God's ways, we are not really capable of fully understanding what life was like in Eden because we have lived in the fallen world for so long. Just as the New Jerusalem, Paradise, God's Kingdom, reflects what life was like in Eden, with the river of Living Water, light flowing abundantly through us all as we walk continuously in God's Presence, life here in the fallen world is so unlike that life, it is as far as is the East is from the West (Psa 103:12, Mat 24:27). But let's reiterate what the creation story told us. Adam and Eve were naked, they had no cover, no need to cover themselves, they were completely open, there was no shame, no pride, no idea of separateness. They were at one with one another and they walked in the Presence of God. It was only after breaking trust with God that the idea of separateness, the need to hide, came into play. Then there was shame and blame. We cannot, of our own will get back into Eden. The way is locked and guarded by a flaming sword. Our relationships cannot be put back together by our will, our determination, our efforts. We must go by God's way. He can open the gate to the Kingdom and to the healing of relationships. Luke 11:9-*10 "And I tell you, ask, and it will be given to you; seek, and you will find; knock, and it will be opened to you. 10 For everyone who asks receives, and the one who seeks finds, and to the one who knocks it will be opened."* Matthew 6:33 *"But seek first the kingdom of God and his righteousness, and all these things will be added to you."*

Man and woman are alike in many ways. But we are also different in a number of ways. Our argument here is that the natural consequences of who we are is reflected in what God knew of our nature and shared with us after we chose poorly. We'll start with Adam's consequences because, as is the nature of man himself, the consequences appear to be more straightforward, simpler. Gen 2:5 *"there was no man to work the ground."* Gen 2:15 *"The Lord God took the man and put him in the garden of Eden to work it and keep it."* The consequences: Gen 3:17-19 *"Because you have listened to the voice of your wife and have eaten of the tree of which*

I commanded you, 'You shall not eat of it,' cursed is the ground because of you; in pain you shall eat of it all the days of your life; thorns and thistles it shall bring forth for you; and you shall eat the plants of the field. By the sweat of your face you shall eat bread, till you return to the ground, for out of it you were taken; for you are dust, and to dust you shall return."

The most obvious consequence is that man was put here to work, and his work was no longer going to be easy. There would be trials and challenges to his assigned task. These challenges would continue right until the time of his death. And he would die and return to dust. In his fallen state, he may not be able to accomplish all that he is assigned to do, his goals in life, before his life ends and he returns to that state in which he was before he was created with a purpose.

There is another less obvious consequence, which is reflected in the statement *"Because you have listened to the voice of your wife"* and done what God commanded him not to do, which brings more complexity into the picture. And, though less obvious, as is true of many paradoxical aspects of God, it is the more important. It points out, again, the prime importance of listening to God, trusting God. It reflects the greatest command, *"Love the Lord your God,"* and it clearly indicates that even though God created male and female in order that there could be relationship, man's primary relationship is to be with God. Our primary task as males is to trust Him, to listen to Him, to obey Him. This is primary before there can be relationship with another person, even a person with whom we have become "one flesh." The spiritual relationship is to be primary before the relationship in the flesh.

Again, Jesus noted that love God and love neighbor were the greatest commands, but the first was love God and the second was love neighbor. With the creation of the miracle of woman came also the miracle of human relationship, relationship reflecting the nature of God (in His image), but nevertheless, less critical than the relationship with God. Why do you think the serpent went for that lie that broke the trust of God? Because that is primary. Upon that trust, all else is built. And if the foundation is not strong, none of the other tasks can be successful. (Luke 6:46-49) And God makes it clear here that He holds man (male) responsible for this foundational relationship. This does not mean that woman is not also to have that relationship with God, indeed it is as critical for her as for man. But God says here, "This is where you fell, Adam. You did not listen to me. You listened to your wife. And even though that human relationship is very strong, as if you are one flesh, still YOU are responsible. It is your job not only to work the earth and seek dominion over it, but I gave the instruction, the command to YOU, and YOU blew it. I hold YOU responsible." He doesn't want our attempts to cover our sins, He doesn't want our pride, our finger-pointing blame; He wants our trust and obedience and He holds Adam responsible. So, here in one respect, we may see, "It's a man's world." His job to make sure the work gets done in spite of obstacles, and his job to be sure that he and the couple are putting God first. Big responsibilities. Big rewards, as well, when we successfully carry out those tasks, not individually, but as they work together as part of the pattern. To be sure, we men have our roles to play in the procreation aspect, and those are fleshed out more later in Scripture. But our approach here of looking at the roles of the sexes based upon the natural consequences of our failure in the Garden puts more of the responsibility of the procreation task squarely on the shoulders of Eve.

So now we get to Eve, the crown of creation, the miracle that allows human relationship, the culmination of God's creating creatures "in our image."

> *Gen 3:16 To the woman he said, "I will surely multiply your pain in childbearing; in pain you shall bring forth children. Your desire shall be for your husband, and he shall rule over you."*

We already know that the physical design of the woman is such that she is the one who bears the children. She has the correct "physical equipment" to carry the offspring and the correct "physical beauty" to attract the man for reproduction. But she is also the one through whom comes human relationship. So, in her nature is the inclination for relationship, the heart for nurture, the propensity for interpersonal interaction. So her consequences fall into this realm. Relationship, partnership are critical for the dominion task to be carried out, to be certain. God saw it was not good before there was relationship. He created woman from man to be just the right combination of spiritual and physical nature to build relationship "in our image." He knew, as triune, what was necessary to make for successful relationship. He created a "matched set," suitable partners, to make it so that the three tasks mankind was given: obedience to God, procreating, and exercising dominion over creation, could be successfully accomplished.

He will *"multiply your pain in childbearing; in pain you shall bring forth children."* Her task, focusing on procreation, will be painful, just as man's work in the soil would be painful. But just as a sense of accomplishment in his tasks are highly important to man, as a part of his nature, and difficulties in that accomplishment cause him pain, so a sense of relationship is highly important to woman. Struggles in those areas that are basic to her nature give her pain. Her nature is one of beauty, of nurture, of relationship. There is not only the actual physical pain of pregnancy and labor, which are very real. There are all the emotional pains, which affect man and woman both, but because she is so relational, the woman more. The natural consequence of that relational nature is the pain when she is rejected by her child as he or she grows, the pain of seeing her child having physical or emotional pain, and the immense pain when one of her offspring dies. Knowing that her action in listening to the serpent has brought an ongoing enmity between her and the serpent, that her offspring are destined to pain in this life, on this earth, is a great source of pain to this relational being. It hits right where her heart is. The consequences fit the nature of the one who receives the consequences.

The second aspect of her consequences is listed as *"Your desire shall be for your husband,"* or some translations say *"Your desire shall be for man."* What is the message here? Part of it is certainly to do with woman's role in procreation, that she would desire his relationship in that they may together serve to multiply humankind. Man also has that desire for woman, which is a drive God has placed in us to allow for the procreative task to be fulfilled. But such desire was not mentioned as a part of Adam's consequences, only for Eve. So what is different about Eve that as a result of her actions, it is pointed out that her desire will be for man? Keep in mind as we discuss this, that the three tasks are not really separate, nor can they be separated one from the other. They are a part of the triune nature of God. All three parts must work together in unison. It is God's nature: it is creation's nature.

The Hebrew word "teshuwqah" desire, longing, craving is from the root word "shuwq" meaning to be abundant, to give abundance to, to overflow. We pointed out some physical differences before, between men and women, differences in beauty, differences in "procreative equipment." Another general difference is in strength, physical strength. Sure, we can all point out exceptions, but on the whole, man's physical strength is well adapted to his major task of provision - the job of working in the soil. Through his strength is made possible the abundance of the bounty coming from the earth. In addition to the desire for man's procreative ability with the two in relationship, this desire could be for his ability to produce abundance for the woman and her offspring.

There is another possible way to look at this aspect of desire, which we've alluded to previously. We see this possible interpretation show itself in that catchy phrase,

"It's a man's world," that we discussed earlier. Here we may see the pride that has become "second nature" (our "first nature" is how God made us, in His image and likeness) for us as we reflect the nature of the "ruler of this world." (John 12:31, 14:30, 16:11) It can be desire for man's position. Again, we might see some of this feeling displayed in our children. "It's not fair!" He got what I didn't get. (Whatever grass it is that we perceive is greener on the other side of the fence.) He was made first! He was in relationship with God first. That puts me in position of second-best. It is a reflection of the enmity between the sexes, which, were we in our "first nature," would not be there.

Can this be another part of why Satan approached the woman? Was there a desire on her part to be first, to be better, to show "him" that she can discover something better or more important than just following those same old guidelines God gave? Let's go back to that narrative for a moment.

> *Gen 3:1 Now the serpent was more crafty than any other beast of the field that the Lord God had made. He said to the woman, "Did God actually say, 'You shall not eat of any tree in the garden'?" 2 And the woman said to the serpent, "We may eat of the fruit of the trees in the garden, 3 but God said, 'You shall not eat of the fruit of the tree that is in the midst of the*

garden, neither shall you touch it, lest you die. '" 4 But the serpent said to the woman, "You will not surely die. 5 For God knows that when you eat of it your eyes will be opened, and you will be like God, knowing good and evil." 6 So when the woman saw that the tree was good for food, and that it was a delight to the eyes, and that the tree was to be desired to make one wise, she took of its fruit and ate, and she also gave some to her husband who was with her, and he ate. 7 Then the eyes of both were opened, and they knew that they were naked. And they sewed fig leaves together and made themselves loincloths.

No question about it the serpent is crafty. He goes for our vulnerabilities. God didn't tell Eve not to partake, He told Adam. That can raise all kinds of questions in Eve, especially if she feels she is in second place. Why did God tell Adam and not me? Did He really say that or what EXACTLY did He say? Did Adam hear it right? Did he tell me EXACTLY what God said? Is Adam making rules and laying them on me? The questions go on... An easy spot for the deceiver to step in is where there is a measure of pride. And pride is that most deadly of sins because it is an inward spiral, separating us more and more from relationship with others and with God.

"It's a man's world." Are you a woman? Does that bother you? Does it just "stick in your craw?" Does it make you feel that life is not fair to you? That is the serpent speaking his favorite lie to you, the pride lie. *"God knows that when you eat of it your eyes will be opened, and you will be like God, knowing good and evil."* Pride does indeed kill.

"It's a man's world." Are you a man? Does that give you just a bit of pride in your status? Are you just a bit haughty that you were first created? Are you proud that you are not a woman? Be careful! The serpent is indeed real and is right here with us. 1 Peter 5:8 *"Be sober-minded; be watchful. Your adversary the devil prowls around like a roaring lion, seeking someone to devour."* He is constantly on the prowl. He loves that one, pride. It was his downfall. He wants to share it with you.

Pride separates the sexes. It makes us no longer be "one flesh." We were not designed to be in competition with one another. We were designed, in the image and likeness of God, for close relationship and with specific tasks in mind. We were each given gifts, and we were each given weaknesses. We work best together as a team. We are "suitable partners" for one another in this quest for dominion over God's creation. We must work together, not at enmity toward one another. And this points back to some of our initial discussion on loving one another as Jesus loved us, sacrificially, putting the other first. That is not easy. In fact, it's downright impossible if we try to do it without God. Remember, we must first love God, and then love our neighbor. *"I can do all things through Christ who strengthens me."* (Phil 4:13)

If you are married and you feel that you and your spouse are in competition on some level, take this feeling to God in prayer, together. This is a very common problem seen in marriage in this age, and it is related to the lies one or both of you have been told by the father of lies. You will need God's help to work through this. A married couple should be facing life's challenges together as a team, with a focus on God's will. If there is competition or conflict within the marriage, Satan's very old tactic of "divide and conquer" is working, which weakens each spouse in the individual life battles that they have, and definitely weakens any challenges to the marriage itself.

There is one more aspect of the consequences of Eve's actions that we must touch on. And this may be the most controversial of all among today's Christians. *"... and he shall rule over you."* That really raises the hackles of some women. Again, we do not have insight into God's purposes, only knowing as much as He shares with us. The Hebrew word "mashal" means to rule or exercise dominion over. There's that dominion word again, man was told to have dominion over the earth, but the word is a different word than the one used in God's explanation of man's role on earth. The word used here is the word that is used of God's dominion over His kingdom. Lest it be unclear, it is not at all within the power of man to exercise dominion over any part of God's creation. We like to point out that when God tells you something in Scripture, you should listen. But when He tells you something over and over again, that is a very clear sign He wants you to pay particular attention to that message. Only in God, through Jesus Christ, is there dominion over creation. (Job 25:2, Psa 8:5-8, 103:22, 145:13, Dan 4:3, 7:13-14, 7:27, Eph 1:17-21, 1 Tim 6:13-16, 1 Pet 4:10-11, 5:11, Jude1:24-25, Rev 1:5-6) Only in God is dominion. You can take that one to the bank!

So what does it mean when David says in Psalm 145 *"...your dominion endures throughout all generations."*? Again we are not Bible scholars, nor gifted with skills to translate Hebrew. But one can get sense of what he may be suggesting from the context of this usage in this song of praise. One gets the sense of "benevolent rule," a loving and caring relationship: Psa 145:10-14 *All your works shall give thanks to you, O LORD, and all your saints shall bless you! They shall speak of the glory of your kingdom and tell of your power, to make known to the children of man your mighty deeds, and the glorious splendor of your kingdom.*

Your kingdom is an everlasting kingdom, and your dominion endures throughout all generations. The LORD is faithful in all his words and kind in all his works. The LORD upholds all who are falling and raises up all who are bowed down.

Is that what God says of Eve's consequence, not in a condescending way or a domineering or dominating way, but in a loving, supportive way? Does He refer to the responsibility that He is giving Adam, to obey and trust in God, and try to convey to Eve that Adam will have that responsibility of assuring the connection with God, obeying Divine will, and that he will help assure that connection for her, as well? If God's will reigns for Adam, he will help assure that God's will reigns for Eve, as well. We have all seen examples in our study of history of benevolent dictators, but more commonly we have seen dictators who are driven by their own desires and own will, rather than God's will. This colors our perception. It all goes back to trusting God, trusting that He loves us unconditionally and knows in each and every circumstance what is best for us. As a result of her lack of trust, an exercising of her pride, she is placed in a more supported situation. If you are a manager in your job and you have an employee who has struggled in some area, is not the path of improvement frequently to be in a position of more support? It is not punitive, but nurturing. Just a question raised, not an answer given.

A reminder from Rev 2:23 – *"And all the churches will know that I am he who searches mind and heart, and I will give to each of you according to your works."* God searches our hearts. He knows our spirit.

Jesus challenges the Pharisees, who are focused on the "works" part of that statement, thinking they are winning their way to God by their good works. He makes it very clear this is NOT what God desires.

Matthew 15:7-9 You hypocrites! Well did Isaiah prophesy of you, when he said:

> *"This people honors me with their lips, but their heart is far from me; in vain do they worship me, teaching as doctrines the commandments of men."*

> Matthew 15:15-20 *But Peter said to him, "Explain the parable to us." And he said, "Are you also still without understanding? Do you not see that whatever goes into the mouth passes into the stomach and is expelled? But what comes out of the mouth proceeds from the heart, and this defiles a person. For out of the heart come evil thoughts, murder, adultery, sexual immorality, theft, false witness, slander. These are what defile a person. But to eat with unwashed*

hands does not defile anyone." The Lord knows our heart, our spirit. As noted before, He desires a humble heart, a contrite spirit.

Psa 111:10 *"Reverence for the LORD is the beginning of wisdom: those who act accordingly have a good understanding; his glory endures forever."*

Reverence is yirah, which can mean reverence, respect, fear, or honor. It comes from the root word yare', to revere, to fear, to honor, to be held in awe.

The Jews say the Shema each day; they for many, many centuries have recognized the importance of loving the Lord and being obedient to Him. They stress that it is to be a part of everything that is done in life.

Deuteronomy 6:4-9

Hear, O Israel: The Lord is our God, the Lord alone. 5 You shall love the Lord your God with all your heart, and with all your soul, and with all your might. 6 Keep these words that I am commanding you today in your heart. 7 Recite them to your children and talk about them when you are at home and when you are away, when you lie down and when you rise. 8 Bind them as a sign on your hand, fix them as an emblem on your forehead, 9 and write them on the doorposts of your house and on your gates.

Matthew 19:16-26 The Rich Young Man

And behold, a man came up to him, saying, "Teacher, what good deed must I do to have eternal life?" And he said to him, "Why do you ask me about what is good? There is only one who is good. If you would enter life, keep the commandments." He said to him, "Which ones?" And Jesus said, "You shall not murder, You shall not commit adultery, You shall not steal, You shall not bear false witness, Honor your father and mother, and, You shall love your neighbor as yourself." The young man said to him, "All these I have kept. What do I still lack?" Jesus said to him, "If you would be perfect, go, sell what you possess and give to the poor, and you will have treasure in heaven; and come, follow me." When the young man heard this he went away sorrowful, for he had great possessions.

And Jesus said to his disciples,

> *"Truly, I say to you, only with difficulty will a rich person enter the kingdom of heaven. Again I tell you, it is easier for a camel to go through the eye of a needle than for a rich person to enter the kingdom of God."*

When the disciples heard this, they were greatly astonished, saying, "Who then can be saved?" But Jesus looked at them and said, "With man this is impossible, but with God all things are possible."

We cannot save ourselves, only God can. Any other thing in this life that we put before God becomes our god. The thing we most desire becomes our downfall. The rich young man had no problem following the other commandments that Jesus put before him. But when Jesus challenged him to give up the thing that on this earth meant the most to him (his "god"), he could not do it. That is how it is with us. It may not be money. It might be the "high" we get from sex or from power or from risk-taking. Whatever means the most to us is our downfall. These in italics, the young man pridefully says he has done. Then Jesus, as always, goes for the zinger. Give up what really means most to you and come to me. Sacrifice what you cling to...

Exodus 20:

> *3"You shall have no other gods before me. 4 "You shall not make for yourself a carved image, 7 "You shall not take the name of the Lord your God in vain, 8 "Remember the Sabbath day, to keep it holy. 12 "Honor your father and your mother. 13 "You shall not murder. 14"You shall not commit adultery. 15 "You shall not steal. 16 "You shall not bear false*

witness against your neighbor. 17 "You shall not covet your neighbor's...

What is the message? The thing that you think is the most important thing in your life is your god, it is what you worship, it is your center. If that god is Yahweh, Jehovah, and you can give up on all else that means most to you, you will enter the Kingdom of God. Other things at the center of our lives keep us separate from God. The Kingdom of God is here and now.

> Luke 17:20-21 *Being asked by the Pharisees when the kingdom of God would come, he answered them,*

> *"The kingdom of God is not coming with signs to be observed, nor will they say, 'Look, here it is! ' or 'There! ' for behold, the kingdom of God is in the midst of you."*

It is a glorious way of living, full of joy, joy that cannot be explained to anyone who has not experienced it. It removes worries, stress, and anxieties. It brings a feeling of being centered. Does this reflect the life you are living? Or do you feel "in competition" with your husband, your wife? Do you feel the "need" to be the top performer at your job? No other area in our lives can fill that desire for intimate connection with our Creator. No person-to-person relationship, no outrageous salary, no fun activity, nothing can fill that desire for connection to God.

Was Eve feeling "second-best" in her relationship with Adam, with God? Was there an enticement that Satan jumped in to fill with his deceit and lies? This is certainly why so much is made of the importance of humility and submitting to the will of God in the Bible. Loving our neighbors. Agape love, loving without expecting to receive in return, putting others ahead of ourselves. And we are weak. We cannot do it on our own we must give ourselves over to the One who can. Humility:

> Luke 9:46-48 46 *An argument arose among them as to which of them was the greatest. 47 But Jesus, knowing the reasoning of their hearts, took a child and put him by his side 48 and said to them, "Whoever receives this child in my name receives me, and whoever receives me receives him who sent me. For he who is least among you all is the one who is great."*

Male / female relationships

There are some serious issues in male - female relationships in relation to the marriages of the fathers: Abraham, Isaac, and Jacob, which we cannot address here, but we encourage you to read. The Bible also in places speaks directly to the topic of marriage and family relationships. These are primarily in the Epistles of Paul, letters written to individuals or churches, often from prison, and often in response to specific circumstances or specific questions in the church.

One of Paul's most famous passages speaks to the topic of agape love. Agapao = love, charity in First Corinthians 13. It is familiar to most everyone. In it, Paul delineates what are the attributes that can be seen, of agape love. It is patient and kind, not envying or boasting, not arrogant or rude, not insisting on one's own way, not irritable or resentful, not rejoicing at wrongdoing, but rejoicing with the truth, bearing all things, believing all things, hoping all things, enduring all things, these qualities never ending. These are qualities that should be apparent in our Christian relationships, especially in marriage.

Paul shares these types of discussions, more lofty and theological, in his letters, and he also includes areas of practical advice in certain letters to churches. Sometimes he will indicate that the ideas shared are his own personal advice, and sometimes that there is guidance from the Lord. He does not indicate this in each circumstance. Some readers of the Bible have difficulties with some of Paul's practical advice. We will try to show how some of his thoughts relate to what we have already shared and other Biblical instances.

An example of a passage where Paul shares his own inclinations, intertwined with those from the Lord, is in 1 Corinthians 7, where he shares some "principles for marriage." In this chapter, it is clear that he is responding to some specific questions, and he throws in plenty of his own personal beliefs: for example "It is good for a man not to have sexual relations with a woman." To argue against this statement, it is quite clear that one of God's primary tasks for man is to be fruitful and multiply. Further, if one but studies the Song of Songs, it is clear that sexual relations are not condemned by God's teaching at all. He does go further and indicate that to him, it is for the appropriate outlet for sexual temptation, that marriage is available. He indicates some marriage principles, which basically indicate that the man and woman should stand on equal ground as far as physical relationship goes (4 For the wife does not have authority over her own body, but the husband does. Likewise the husband does not have authority over his own body, but the wife does.) He also suggests in verse 7 that he is celibate and that he wishes that all could be so, yet if one cannot exercise self-control, then marriage is available. God clearly established the marriage relationship and said *"It is not good for man to be alone."* Thus, while God would certainly not condemn someone choosing celibacy, neither would it be the Lord's desire, as Paul's that all could be celibate. Several times he indicates what he, Paul says, and one time what the Lord says, not him. In each such reading one must always go back to whether a message is consistent with what God has told us otherwise. (Hebrews 13:8) *"Jesus Christ is the same yesterday, today, and forever."*

We are called to be discerning (Matthew 10:16 *"Behold, I am sending you out as sheep in the midst of wolves, so be wise as serpents and innocent as doves."*) and to test the spirit of what we are being told.

1 John 4:1-3 Test the Spirits

> *Beloved, do not believe every spirit, but test the spirits to see whether they are from God, for many false prophets have gone out into the world. By this you know the Spirit of God: every spirit that confesses that Jesus Christ has come in the flesh is from God, and every spirit that does not confess Jesus is not from God. This is the spirit of the antichrist, which you heard was coming and now is in the world already.*

The Sprit of Truth, as pointed out to us by the Apostle John, is the Holy Spirit.

John 16:13-15

When the Spirit of truth comes, he will guide you into all the truth, for he will not speak on his own authority, but whatever he hears he will speak, and he will declare to you the things that are to come. He will glorify me, for he will take what is mine and declare it to you. All that the Father has is mine; therefore I said that he will take what is mine and declare it to you.

We can only understand the message of scripture if we delve into it and if we have a guide. Acts 8:29-31 *And the Spirit said to Philip, "Go over and join this chariot." So Philip ran to him and heard him reading Isaiah the prophet and asked, "Do you understand what you are reading?" And he said, "How can I, unless someone guides me?" And he invited Philip to come up and sit with him.*

We remind you of the initial chapter on "understanding." We must be cautious not to focus on one "favorite scripture" that reflects exactly what we believe and neglect many others that might soften the impact of that one scripture. We must seek the guidance of the Lord, both through study of the scripture, and by asking Him to guide us, he brings the Spirit of Truth to guide us.

Psalm 25:4-5

Make me to know your ways, O Lord; teach me your paths. Lead me in your truth and teach me, for you are the God of my salvation; for you I wait all the day long.

1 Corinthians 2:6-16 Wisdom from the Spirit

Yet among the mature we do impart wisdom, although it is not a wisdom of this age or of the rulers of this age, who are doomed to pass away. But we impart a secret and hidden wisdom of God, which God decreed before the ages for our glory. None of the rulers of this age understood this, for if they had, they would not have crucified the Lord of glory. But, as it is written,

"What no eye has seen, nor ear heard, nor the heart of man imagined, what God has prepared for those who love him"—

these things God has revealed to us through the Spirit. For the Spirit searches everything, even the depths of God. For who knows a person's thoughts except the spirit of that person, which is in him? So also no one comprehends the thoughts of God except the Spirit of God. Now we have received not the spirit of the world, but the Spirit who is from God, that we might understand the things freely given us by God. 13 And we impart this in words not taught by human wisdom but taught by the Spirit, interpreting spiritual truths to those who are spiritual. The natural person does not accept the things of the Spirit of God, for they are folly to him, and he is not able to understand them because they are spiritually discerned. The spiritual person judges all things, but is himself to be judged by no one. "For who has understood the mind of the Lord so as to instruct him?" But we have the mind of Christ.

In Ephesians, chapter 5, Paul encourages us all, male and female, to put away malice, bitterness, wrath, anger, slander and clamor. He encourages us all to be imitators of God, to be kind to one another, tenderhearted, forgiving one another, walking in love and giving up self for one another, walking as children of light, trying to discern what is pleasing to the Lord. He says we should be filled with the Spirit, singing spiritual songs to one another, being thankful in all things to God, and submitting to one another. We are all to relate to one another, men and women alike, in submission, out of reverence for Christ.

Then he proceeds to talk about some of the hierarchical structures that God has set. In particular, he speaks about the hierarchical structure of the family.

Ephesians 5:22-33 Wives and Husbands

Wives, submit to your own husbands, as to the Lord. For the husband is the head of the wife even as Christ is the head of the church, his body, and is himself its

Savior. Now as the church submits to Christ, so also wives should submit in everything to their husbands.

Husbands, love your wives, as Christ loved the church and gave himself up for her, that he might sanctify her, having cleansed her by the washing of water with the word, so that he might present the church to himself in splendor, without spot or wrinkle or any such thing, that she might be holy and without blemish. In the same way husbands should love their wives as their own bodies. He who loves his wife loves himself. For no one ever hated his own flesh, but nourishes and cherishes it, just as Christ does the church, because we are members of his body. "Therefore a man shall leave his father and mother and hold fast to his wife, and the two shall become one flesh." This mystery is profound, and I am saying that it refers to Christ and the church. However, let each one of you love his wife as himself, and let the wife see that she respects her husband.

The Greek word for submitting is hypotasso, which means a voluntary attitude of giving in, cooperating, assuming responsibility, and carrying a burden. Recall we talked about God having given the responsibility to the husband for seeking after and maintaining the relationship with God, and as it was worded, that the husband would "rule over" the wife. And Paul notes that the two joining and becoming "one flesh" is a profound mystery. It is a hierarchical structure, a system of responsibility established by God. As we have noted before, His ways are not our ways. We cannot understand them all. But for marriage to work as He designed it to work, we would follow His design. Likely very few marriages in this age follow this structure: a strong relationship, a guiding relationship by the Father's will, both husband and wife submitting to God's will, and then when both are submitted to God's will, if there is a difference of approach, the woman respecting the authority that God placed in the hands of the man. With fifty percent of marriages failing, our perspective is that it is amazing that as many as half make it in this age, for surely a much smaller percent today follow this structure. Marriages last for differing reasons, but if they are truly based upon God's guidance, marriage will accomplish its goal in moving toward the tasks God has assigned to mankind.

This is not to say that if the wife is a Godly woman and the husband is not, that she is to accede to his demands in all circumstances. This is not at all the message of the Bible. We must test the spirits, we must discern, we must seek God's guidance in all things. The story of David, Abigail and Nabal in 1 Samuel 25 bring some clarity to Paul's exhortation that the woman should submit *"in everything to their husbands."* Abigail followed God's will in the circumstance with David and his men, and her husband Nabal was not apparently acting in God's will, Abigail discerned a better way and saved lives. God is the one to whom we all should submit *"in everything;"* if there is ever conflict that would put God's will second, the choice should clearly be made in God's will. This is a pretty clear example.

Paul addresses this partially in 1 Corinthians 7:12-16 *"To the rest I say (I, not the Lord) that if any brother has a wife who is an unbeliever, and she consents to live with him, he should not divorce her. 13 If any woman has a husband who is an unbeliever, and he consents to live with her, she should not divorce him. 14 For the unbelieving husband is made holy because of his wife, and the unbelieving wife is made holy because of her husband. Otherwise your children would be unclean, but as it is, they are holy. 15 But if the unbelieving partner separates, let it be so. In such cases the brother or sister is not enslaved. God has called you to peace. 16 For how do you know, wife, whether you will save your husband? Or how do you know, husband, whether you will save your wife?"*

Both partners in marriage are to put God first. His will is to be sought and adhered to. If both seek God's will, it is unusual that there will be differing approaches in life's decisions. In the unusual circumstance that there is a different perspective, both feeling they are seeing God's will, the first step would be to wait, as God may give the clear answer. If not, after waiting, God's structure is that one must decide, and He has placed the responsibility for this discernment on the male. Perhaps He saw the female as better able to submit, perhaps God felt in that circumstance that the less relational mind was necessary to make a decision. We cannot know all the ways of God. All we can do is go by His inspired Word. This is a picture of how marriage was designed to work: supporting, sacrificing, considering the other, without pride, looking first to God and patiently awaiting His guidance.

Scripture

A stronger word of caution about Scripture and how it is used. We are human, we are fallible, we tend to take all good things that our generous God gives to us and turn it to our own uses. The Bible tells a consistent story throughout, of the great love affair of God for His people. Jesus Christ is the center of all Scripture. Scripture has been used throughout the ages in horrific ways. It has been used as a weapon in bludgeoning peoples and those of other religions (examples: indigenous peoples in many countries, the Crusades). It has been used as a temptation (even the devil used scripture: Mat 4:5-6). It has been used to establish certain groups in a position of power over others. Jesus's times of greatest passion were when He spoke against the misuse of Scripture by the Pharisees: (Matthew 23:2-7) *"The scribes and the Pharisees sit on Moses 'seat, so practice and observe whatever they tell you— but not what they do. For they preach, but do not practice. They tie up heavy burdens, hard to bear, and lay them on people's shoulders, but they themselves are not willing to move them with their finger. They do all their deeds to be seen by others. For they make their phylacteries broad and their fringes long, and they love the place of honor at feasts and the best seats in the synagogues and greetings in the marketplaces and being called rabbi by others."*

I know good Christian people who have selected out their "favorite scripture" and held onto it and made it their "god" and used it against their spouses to the detriment of their marriage. Four examples come to mind very quickly:

I know a man who destroyed his relationship with his wife by clinging to (1 Corinthians 7:4-5) *"For the wife does not have authority over her own body, but the husband does. Likewise the husband does not have authority over his own body, but the wife does. Do not deprive one another, except perhaps by agreement for a limited time, that you may devote yourselves to prayer; but then come together again, so that Satan may not tempt you because of your lack of self- control."* He drove a wedge between himself and his wife with this scriptural weapon.

I know a woman who used this scripture as a weapon: (Ephesians 4:26) *"Be angry and do not sin; do not let the sun go down on your anger..."* She used that to torment her husband at bedtime, unloading all her frustrations at the time of settling down for the night.

I know a man who could not stand his wife's constant nagging and chose to separate himself from her: (Proverbs 21:9) *"It is better to live in a corner of the housetop than in a house shared with a quarrelsome wife."*

I know several men who selected this as their favorite verse, to 'abuse' their wives: (Ephesians 5:24) *"Now as the church submits to Christ, so also wives should submit in everything to their husbands."*

If any of these examples make you angry, that someone could do this to another person, we say to you, *"Let he who is without sin cast the first stone."* We must all look to our own hearts and seek God in every situation.

The Bible is a consistent story about God's love for His people and how we are to love one another. As Jesus noted, in Matthew 22:37-40 And he said to him, *"You shall love the Lord your God with all your heart and with all your soul and with all your mind. This is the great and first commandment. And a second is like it: You shall love your neighbor as yourself. On these two commandments depend all the Law and the Prophets."*

Even when Jesus is rejected, He does not use His power against others: (Luke 9:53-55) *But the people did not receive him, because his face was set toward Jerusalem. And when his disciples James and John saw it, they said, "Lord, do you want us to tell fire to come down from heaven and consume them?" But he turned and rebuked them.*

We cannot separate out our favorite verse to use against others. It is a guide, together with the wisdom and discernment from the Holy Spirit, to live the life that God intended for us, to give us dominion over this earth, this age. It is a story of love, agape love.

Concluding comments

The structure of God's world is arranged in patterns; it is hierarchical and interactive. Much is made about obedience and respect for authority. Paul clearly recognizes the interdependence of male and female. 1 Corinthians 11:11-12 *"Nevertheless, in the Lord woman is not independent of man nor man of woman; 12 for as woman was made from man, so man is now born of woman. And all things are from God."* All things are from God. Once again, it must all be centered on our trust in God, our faith in God.

Micah 7:7

But as for me, I will look to the Lord;

I will wait for the God of my salvation;

my God will hear me.

Philippians 4:19

"And my God will supply every need of yours according to his riches in glory in Christ Jesus."

Romans 8:31-32 God's Everlasting Love

"What then shall we say to these things? If God is for us, who can be against us? He who did not spare his own Son but gave him up for us all, how will he not also with him graciously give us all things?"

We must have faith that He knows what is best for us. We must have faith that the Creator of all that we see and feel and hear and experience knows how this Creation best works. We must believe that He leads us in the paths that are best for us. We must have faith. Faith means placing trust in another's authority in the circumstance, respect for that authority.

If we cannot have faith and respect in God, and in one another, we cannot fulfill His task of having dominion over this earth and reconnecting with God in paradise. We must together seek Him, we must submit our own wills. We must be humble. We must let Him take the reins of our lives. We must be wise and discerning, and willing to turn the authority over to the one to whom it belongs.

Whose authority will you trust?

Luke 4:5-6 *And the devil took him up and showed him all the kingdoms of the world in a moment of time, and said to him, "To you I will give all this authority and their glory, for it has been delivered to me, and I give it to whom I will."*

> Matthew 28:18-20 *And Jesus came and said to them, "All authority in heaven and on earth has been given to me. Go therefore and make disciples of all nations, baptizing them in the name of the Father and of the Son and of the Holy Spirit, teaching them to observe all that I have commanded you. And behold, I am with you always, to the end of the age."*

We cannot tell you the why the world is as it is, except that God's way is most often a way of paradoxes. But we do see a clear pattern, and patterns are what this little book is about: Patterns of God. Many times He told us the last will be first and the first, last.

Whether it be rich and poor, male and female, race versus race, religion versus religion, we are faced with dichotomies, choices to be made. We are given the freedom to choose. But we are given guidance. (Luke 10:27) *"And he answered, 'You shall love the Lord your God with all your heart and with all your soul and with all your strength and with all your mind, and your neighbor who is like unto yourself.'"*

Note that the Lord does put us to the test in life. (Exodus 15:5)*"... There the LORD made for them a statute and a rule, and there he tested them..."* (See also Exo 16:4 and Exo 20:20) Pride is the challenge, the test. Whether we feel better than our neighbor and therefore privileged, or whether we feel lesser than our neighbor and therefore deserving of recompense, each side of the dichotomy must overcome pride, which is the focus on self. We cannot, of ourselves do this. We failed in the Garden. Adam failed Eve. Eve failed Adam. They both failed God. We fail every day. But thankfully, God is full of grace, and God does not fail. (Mark 10:27) *"Jesus looked at them and said, 'With man it is impossible, but not with God. For all things are possible with God.'"* The Good News is that we cannot do it, but He can. And all we must do is give it ALL to Him. And, (Philippians 4:13) *"I can do all things through him who strengthens me."*

It is all about our willingness to humble ourselves. This is the test for the woman: if her life is harder, can she still humble herself before the man? This is the test for the man:

if he is in a position over the woman, can he still humble himself and love her sacrificially? Plug in any dichotomous relationship: races, riches, religions... this is the test of this world... (Matthew 7:1-2) Judging Others - *1 "Judge not, that you be not judged. 2 For with the judgment you pronounce you will be judged, and with the measure you use it will be measured to you."*

Do you have your favorite scripture? Do you use it to better yourself? Do you use it to inspect the speck in your neighbor's eye while you have a log in yours? Humble yourself, turn it over to God. He will guide you by way of the Holy Spirit. Do you struggle with this? Is it hard to put "self" out of your mind? The disciples struggled with this concept though they walked with Him (or perhaps because they walked with Him?) (Mark 9:33-35) *And they came to Capernaum. And when he was in the house he asked them, "What were you discussing on the way?" But they kept silent, for on the way they had argued with one another about who was the greatest. And he sat down and called the twelve. And he said to them, "If anyone would be first, he must be last of all and servant of all."*

It is repeated many times, (Matthew 20:16) *"So the last will be first, and the first last."* How we all struggle with this concept. This is the very test of this world. It is a world of relationship designed by a God of relationship. And as long as we focus on our "self," relationship will suffer. When we focus on "other," we receive what we would strive for paradoxically. When we truly focus on "other," with no ulterior motive, no hidden agenda, no "favorite scripture," relationship grows and the Kingdom grows like a mustard seed.

Is it by "coincidence" that Mary Magdalene was first to witness the Lord after His resurrection? Was it by "coincidence" that it is by way of a Samaritan woman who has had five husbands (see John 4) that many in the Samaritan town are saved? If you are in first place, sell all that you have, give to the poor and follow Him (that is, humble yourself, leave the false god of your superiority). If you are in last place, do not strive to be in first or to bring down the first. Rest assured you are blessed, praise Him and follow Him. You should have great hope. Love God, love your neighbor, and be humble. The paradoxical message is so unlike the message of this world. In all things, we must take up our cross. He showed the way. The message is consistent throughout.

The message is in the Song of Praise (Magnificent) of the Virgin Mary, [of course, also a woman] (Luke 1:51-52)

"He has shown strength with his arm; he has scattered the proud in the thoughts of their hearts; he has brought down

the mighty from their thrones and exalted those of humble estate"

Amen

Every promise of God is an invitation to a fight. He only guarantees the victory when we are committed to fight to the end.

Secret 12

The Kingdom is at War

The state of war

One thing we must always keep in our spirit is the reality of the war in which we are involved. Many Christians, after some time in the faith, when we understand the sacrifice of Jesus, how He paid the entire price for us, when we understand that all was accomplished, finished at the cross, enter into a rest. A misunderstanding of the finished work of Jesus could be catastrophic for the journey. Jesus gave us all authority and power. He will never come back to use it in our place. Jesus gave us the victory. That means he engaged us in a fight because there is no victory without a fight. Many of us are still thinking they have no part to play in taking possession of what Jesus has done for us. This is a great lie of the devil. Jesus gave us authority because we need it, and we must use it.

'Behold, I give you the authority to trample on serpents and scorpions, and over all the power of the enemy, and nothing shall by any means hurt you.'

Luke 10:19

The reason Jesus would give us such authority is because we need it in our earthly journey. The Devil hates all that we have. He hates all that brings joy and happiness. He wants the worst for all of us that have been redeemed by the blood of the Lamb.

When I read the Old Testament and the promises God gave to the children of Israel about Canaan, I was shocked to discover all the battles they had to go through to enter into the Promised Land, Canaan. I always ask myself why did they have to die for something that has been freely promised by God? Why did they have to fight for it? The truth is they had to fight to get in.

We must understand the implication of what Joshua said, leading the people of Israel to the Promised Land. At one moment in the journey to Canaan, seven tribes had not yet received their inheritance and Joshua said to the children of Israel:

> *"How long will you neglect to go and possess the land which the LORD God of your fathers has given you?"*
>
> *Joshua 18:3*

Why do they have to fight for something God has given? This is the secret:

Every promise of God is an invitation to a fight. He only guarantees the victory when we are committed to fight to the end.

Throughout the Old Testament, God makes covenants with His people, Israel. Each time, there is a promise from God, and an expectation of His people; a promise from His people and an expectation of their God. God keeps His promises; we are weak and do not. But he makes it clear that He is always there to help us fulfill our part of the covenant if we will just trust Him, turn it over to Him. I love the story in Judges where God calls Gideon to defeat an enemy of His people. Gideon amasses 32,000 men to defeat the enemy. God does not want the Israelites to fight with 32,000 men, because He knows the nature of man, who will claim that the Victory was of his own doing. Instead, God winnows the fighters to three hundred, so that the people will understand that the Victory belongs to God (see especially Judges 7). We must be prepared to fight, but we must also trust that if we love God with all our heart, mind, soul and strength (Mark 12:30, the First Commandment), He will provide the Victory.

The Old Testament is a foreshadowing of the New Testament. Today we are still fighting but it is not a physical fight anymore. Paul explains it better writing to the Ephesians:

> *Put on the whole armor of God, that you may be able to stand against the wiles of the devil. For we do not wrestle against flesh and blood, but against principalities, against powers, against the rulers of the darkness of this age, [and] against spiritual [hosts] of wickedness in the heavenly [places].*
>
> *Ephesians 6: 11-12*

Our family, ministries, friends, job, everything we do and everything we love are constantly under attack. Jesus will put it this way:

"Assuredly, I say to you, among those born of women there has not risen one greater than John the Baptist; but he who is least in the kingdom of heaven is greater than he. "And from the days of John the Baptist until now **the kingdom of heaven suffers violence, and the violent take it by force***."*

Mat 11:11-12

Our destiny will never come to us without our moving toward it. There is a devilish believe today that leads people to wait for dreams to come to them. It is only when we agree to fight that we will take possession of what has been given to us. We must fight to keep the WORD. The must fight for our marriages, we must fight for our family. We must fight to keep our joy, happiness. We must fight to live pain free and harm free life. To manifest the promises of God, we must fight. We cannot do it alone, without God's help, but He does not give it to us without our effort at keeping the covenant, carrying out our part of the bargain.

The Parable of the Rich Young Man is very instructive (Mark 10:17-27). Jesus calls for the man to fight a great inner battle,

And Jesus, looking at him, loved him, and said to him, "You lack one thing: go, sell all that you have and give to the poor, and you will have treasure in

heaven; and come, follow me." Disheartened by the saying, he went away sorrowful, for he had great possessions.   *10:21-22*

And Jesus looked around and said to his disciples, "How difficult it will be for those who have wealth to enter the kingdom of God!" And the disciples were amazed at his words. But Jesus said to them again, "Children, how difficult it is to enter the kingdom of God!   *10:23-24*

And they were exceedingly astonished, and said to him, "Then who can be saved?" Jesus looked at them and said, "With man it is impossible, but not with God. For all things are possible with God."

10:26-27

We must be prepared to fight, but we must also know that God fights with us.   *"I can do all things through Christ, who strengthens me."*   *(Phi 4:13)*

At the end of every letter that Jesus sent to the Seven Churches in the book of Revelation, Jesus always concluded by saying:

"To him who overcomes…"

We can overcome because He paid the price. The victory is not possible without Christ, now we can fight because he overcame to give us victory in the battle.

These are the very last words of Jesus in the book of Revelation, given to John the apostle that concluded the bible:

> *"He who overcomes shall inherit all things, and I will be his God and he shall be My son. But the cowardly, unbelieving, abominable, murderers, sexually immoral, sorcerers, idolaters, and all liars shall have their part in the lake which burns with fire and brimstone, which is the second death."*
>
> *Rev 21:7-8*

These are the very last words of Jesus to the all churches, to the saint, the elect and the redeemed. It is a great mistake to believe we do not have to fight anymore. The good news is: we have all we need to be victorious. I could even say more that all we need.

> *You are of God, little children, and you have overcome them, because He who is in you is greater than he who is in the world.*   *1Jn 4:4*

The ground in which we must use our authority is faith in the Victory. There is no power greater than what we have received. The greatness of the power we have received surpasses all the power of the enemy, the devil.

When I came to Christ, as the first person to believe in the family, my family believed I entered into a secret society, or an "occult sect." A year later, my brother came to Christ and soon after my father. My mother had a great concern about the situation of the family. She was afraid, and she secretly decided to consult a native witch doctor. I told you of this story earlier. When she realized there is a secure place inaccessible by magicians, she ran to Christ. In the occult is the realm of Satan. Satan has power over us, but has no power over Christ.

Many of us do not realize who we are in Christ and are still suffering from that ignorance. This is the confession I devised to use frequently, sometimes daily and loudly to remind me of who I truly am:

I am an elect of God: I am elect according to the foreknowledge of God the Father, in sanctification of the Spirit, for obedience and sprinkling of the blood of Jesus Christ. 1 Pet 1:2

I am a child of the living God: I have received Jesus, I believe in His name and He gave the right to become a child of God, John 1:12

I am dead in Christ: I was buried with Jesus in baptism; I was also raised with Him through faith in the working of God, who raised Him from the dead. Col 2:12

I have been Crucified with Christ: I have been crucified with Christ; it is no longer I who live, but Christ lives in me; and the life which I now live in the flesh I live by faith in the Son of God, who loved me and gave Himself for me. Gal 2:20

I am from a royal priesthood: I am a chosen generation, a royal priesthood, a holy nation, His own special people, that I may proclaim the praises of Him who called me out of darkness into His marvelous light; 1 Pe 2:9

I am a flame of fire: I am a minister of the Gospel. I am a flame of fire. Heb 1:7

I am an ambassador of Christ: I am an ambassador of Christ in chains; I must speak boldly, as I ought to speak. Eph 6:20

I am a dwelling place of God: In Jesus, I am edified to be a dwelling place of God in the Spirit. Eph 2:22

I am the light of the world: I am the light of the world. I am set on the holy mountain of God. I cannot be hidden. Mat 5:14

I am invested with authority and power: I have authority to trample on serpents and scorpions, and over all the power of the enemy, and nothing shall by any means hurt me. Luk 10:19 Whatever I bind on earth will be bound in heaven, and whatever I loose on earth will be loosed in heaven. Mat 18:18

I am sited in heavenly places: When I was dead in my trespasses, God made me alive with Christ. God saved me by grace and raised me up, and made me sit in the heavenly places in Christ Jesus, Eph: 5-6

I am redeemed from the curse of the law: Christ has redeemed me from the curse of the law, having become a curse for me. Gal 3:13

I am delivered from the power of darkness: Jesus has delivered me from the power of darkness and translated me into the kingdom of the Son of His love, Col 1:13

I am washed, sanctified and justified: I was washed, I was sanctified, I was justified in the name of the Lord Jesus and by the Spirit of my God. 1 Cor 6-11

I am a king: He has made me king and priest unto God and his Father. Rev 1:6

Understanding who we are and where we are positioned is fundamental for the battle. We have all we need to overcome all obstacles we are facing. We are fighting because we know who we are. We are fighting because we cannot accept or settle for less than what Jesus has provided for us. Because we do not see, we fear. Open our eyes, Lord to see Your power.

When the servant of the man of God rose early in the morning and went out, behold, an army with horses and chariots was all round the city. And the servant said, "Alas, my master! What shall we do?" He said, "Do not be afraid, for those who are with us are more than those who are with them." Then Elisha prayed and said, "O Lord, please open his eyes that he may see." So the Lord opened the eyes of the young man, and he saw, and behold, the mountain was full of horses and chariots of fire all round Elisha.

2 Kings 6:15-17

We are fighting because we know we have the victory:

But thanks be to God, who gives us the victory through our Lord Jesus Christ.   *1 Cor 15:57*

But thanks be to God, who gives us the victory through our Lord Jesus Christ.   1 Cor 15:57

SECRET 12: THE STATE OF WAR

SECRET 12: THE STATE OF WAR

Visit Us @:

www.bibledisciples.org

www.ingramcontent.com/pod-product-compliance
Lightning Source LLC
Chambersburg PA
CBHW061820040426
42447CB00012B/2741